ROCK OF RECOVERY

RELATIONSHIP ADDICTIONS

Christian Enabler/Addiction Recovery

Angie Meadows

And the very God of peace sanctify you wholly; and I pray God your whole spirit and soul and body be preserved blameless unto the coming of our Lord Jesus Christ. 1 Thessalonians 5:23

Study based on the NIV version. KJV verses are identified.

A Thousand Tears, LLC
PO Box 1373
Huntington, WV 25715
enablersjourney@gmail.com
rockofrecovery.com
enablersjourney.com

Table of Contents

INTRODUCTION

The first standard is love.

The second standard is do no harm.

This book is meant to encourage us to build a strong relationship with ourselves and then find healthy family and friends. We can do this when we are educated on toxic behavior patterns. When we can identify the confusion and the lies surrounding us, we can break free.

Some of us have never known healthy loving relationships and don't know how to move forward. The Rock of Recovery series grounds us in principle-based thinking and the foundation of rock-solid ground beneath our feet.

A broken inner world leads to broken relationships. Insecurity and codependency develop quicksand beneath our feet, and we struggle to develop a healthy identity. This book helps us identify the root causes and our associated behaviors and gives us the permission to break dysfunctional cycles.

Interdependency with others is a healthy give and take. This type of relationship grows, matures and endures the test of time.

Then there are four levels of toxic relationships. These relationships always cause suffering and are only sustainable with great sacrifice.

This work is subjective and not scientific. It has been developed over decades of observation of toxic relationships. You may have gone to a half-dozen counselors who look at you like you have two heads. The depth of depravity of relationship addictions are great suffering and internal confusion with external chaos. I hear your pain and give you this book in response. May you grow, mature and heal and have the power to choose healthy relationships.

Forgive me for making up my own terminology on some behaviors. When I teach this information to those in recovery, they ask me if I am in their heads or watching their lives in a movie. Often, those with substance use disorder are struggling emotionally and without relationship recovery cannot find stability.

RELATIONSHIP ADDICTIONS

1) **Codependency** means we give up power to gain power.

2) **Relational dependency** means we are so engrossed with someone else's well-being that we forget about our own. We also may give up our financial power to this relationship.

3) **Trauma bonding** is a lack of our own personal identity. We will compulsively repeat dysfunctional relationship patterns to achieve someone else's approval. Excuse making and rationalizing why this is a good relationship is common. We have been deceived so long, that now we deceive ourselves.

4) **Relational Bondage** is always toxic. It is abuse on steroids. The victim has no identity and is an extention of their abuser. **This person will metaphorically sit in a burning house and swear the house isn't on fire. Martyring themselves for another is common but is of no use. The abusive partner has acquired a good slave. There is no equality or respect unless it is to deceive you to return**

to the cycle of abuse. I would describe this bondage as compulsively returning to verbal, physical, emotional, financial, sexual, or spiritual abuse.

Root Issue: *A person does not have their own identity and cannot love themselves, so they cannot be fully available and love another with a safe connection. They do not possess an internal safe place or self-awareness and are incapable of self-regulation. They usually were previously abused and will settle for crumbs of attention and call it love and devotion.*

Advice: Never give up your personal power. Always maintain or regain your financial independence. Then when you stay in the relationship, it is for the right motives and not because you have no means to escape.

Recovering addicts cannot have casual sex because of abandonment issues. They do not have enough self-control to wait for a relationship to develop at a safe pace. They cannot maintain their own identity because they haven't developed it, or it has been developed in a skewed manner. Therefore, they are still emerging in the development of their identity like immature teenagers.

Emotional development is often arrested at the time of trauma. This trauma could be one major event or a long-term instability during childhood. It could range from parents being unavailable, abusive, or to making the child entitled to do whatever they feel like doing without any normal internal restraints.

A child who is catered to and always pacified emotionally and allowed to indulge emotions with exaggeration will be shocked, irritated, and even disgruntled when adulthood demands them to be responsible.

So, a lack of safety, stability, protection, provisions, or being over protected, or over indulged, are both unhealthy and may develop long term issues in the development of character and emotional stability.

This book will build an awareness of relationship problems and offer some solutions. Healthy relationship foundations that were not developed in childhood will have to be intentionally developed as an adult through self-education and personal growth. May you have the courage to examine every piece of suffering in your life and move toward maturity and healing.

PRINCIPLES

1. Healthy relationships are intentional.
2. People in toxic relationships give power away to gain power and control over another.
3. If I am not content alone, I will never be content with another person.
4. Healthy relationships require emotional fitness.
5. Perversion of truth is manipulation.
6. Obsession is magnetically strong but is **not** love.
7. Relationship addictions suck the life out of you.
8. Addictive relationships never bring health or healing.
9. Painful relationships need distance to bring peace and perspective.
10. Self-absorption misses true love and drops into lust.
11. A wounded inner core develops a fantasy to escape reality and ends in disgrace.
12. True love is never dominance, control, or manipulation.
13. I cannot love another until I can love myself.
14. Healthy love lets us come and go and rejoices in our individuality.
15. Infidelity is reckless and will contaminate your life.

16. Healing toxic thinking and relationship patterns makes space to develop healthy relationship skills.
17. If I agree with lies, I empower the liar.
18. It takes two whole healthy people to make one lasting happy marriage.
19. A lack of identity and self-worth creates internal chaos which will be acted out externally in relationships.
20. Casual sex clouds your judgment and attracts toxic relationships.
21. God loves the broken.
22. Jesus, friend of sinners.

LESSON 1

HEALTHY RELATIONSHIPS

Healthy relationships are intentional.

Introduction

Is there such a thing as a healthy relationship? Yes, there is, but it requires me to be whole. Think of the goals you want for your relationships and plan accordingly. Healthy relationships require continual interpersonal growth and good communication skills.

Knowing a person is a certain way with specific limitations is one thing. Radically accepting it is another. Toxic relationships can improve if one person will work on themselves. As one grows and sets up boundaries, the other one may also. The relationship will really improve if both partners work on themselves.

It is when I need nothing from the relationship to identify and fulfill me that I can let go of trying to fix another person. It is me that needs to work on me. As I focus my attention on a battle within my control, I can grow. I can heal. I become less needy, clingy, and controlling. Then I can decide to stay or leave and either way I will be fine.

If I do not have a strong identity within myself, I will find a need to develop my identity in a relationship with someone else which will always make the relationship unstable. An identity in someone else moves my focus to appeasing and pleasing another and denying my own needs. Or consuming and controlling of another to make sure they are dependent on me and cannot leave. This can cause me to stay in a toxic or an abusive relationship too long.

Here are some healthy relationship goals.

HEALTHY RELATIONSHIP REVIEW

1) **Respect of boundaries - If I am not free to say "No", I will never be free to say "Yes**". Practice respecting the boundaries of your loved one. A healthy relationship needs to ebb and flow, enjoy unity and togetherness as well as open healthy relationships with others. Secondary relationships need to complement your primary relationships. There are several good books and resources on

Lesson

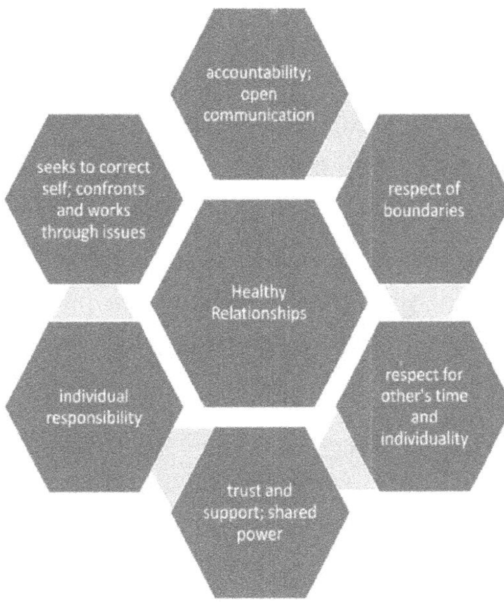

accountability; open communication
respect of boundaries
respect for other's time and individuality
trust and support; shared power
individual responsibility
seeks to correct self; confronts and works through issues
Healthy Relationships

boundaries. If you have ever been abandoned, neglected, abused, or had your own addiction issues, much work will need to be done in this area. If there is confusion in a relationship, work to develop your own boundaries and respect other's boundaries. If you set a boundary, it needs to be within your power to enforce it. If you have given your power away and your boundaries are not respected, work to regain your independence. Empowerment comes through development of a strong identity of what you will and will not tolerate.

2) **Respect for other's time and individuality** - **No relationship**

is healthy without the ability to be an individual with our own personality. I need to know where I start and where I end. If someone is always telling me what to think, eat, wear, say or do, I have lost my identity. Possessing my own identity is my individuality (likes and dislikes) and the ability to make my own decisions. **Healthy relationships are giving and taking.** They are a uniting of oneness and yet allowing everyone to have their own uniqueness. It is a respecting of another person's likes and dislikes. Both individuals in a healthy relationship will often yield their preferences to please the other. This yielding needs to be reciprocal.

3) **Trust, support, and shared power - There is no safe relationship without "trust".** If you cannot trust a companion, could you be with an enemy and not a devoted friend and lover? Support takes on different shapes: financial, physical, emotional, and spiritual. This too is reciprocal. If it is lop-sided, one may dominate in power and control. The other will feel frustrated and unloved.

4) **Individual responsibility - Serving one another without expectation brings great joy.** When both people within a relationship are evenly pulling the weight of the workload, the job becomes enjoyable. Think of yoked oxen. They must be evenly matched, or they will be chaffed, sore or even injured.

5) **Seeks to correct self; confronts and works through issues - A teachable attitude intentionally seeks advise, instruction and**

counsel. When I can recognize and name my personal struggles, I can plan to change. When I am unable to change and keep falling back into dysfunctional patterns, I can be personally proactive and responsible to reach for outside counsel and accountability. Soon, I can discover the root issues and progress towards recovery. When the person I am with is safe to confront without taking an offense, things can be carefree, open, and growing. **Without the treasure of having a person in my life that genuinely cares about what I think, bitterness can fester like annoying splinters.**

6) **Accountability; open communication - Secrets in healthy loving relationships are surprises for holidays and secret gifts.** The relationship can never reach its full potential if you are hiding something, lying, or pretending. **The consequences of hiding and lying is a pervasive feeling of loneliness.** It is better to communicate regularly with your loved one. Let your partner hold you accountable in your weak areas. Ask for accountability (with a dash of grace, of course).

> *If your partner uses your desire for accountability and open communication as a leverage to dominate you, find another trusted, safe person with whom you can develop accountability.*

Also, some people lack insight into their own selves and can be *emotionally illiterate*. Communication gives them so much anxiety that they play avoidance games. This person can be emotionally unavailable and feel distant. Possibly they could be encouraged to work on their *communication skills*. Suggest counseling for them to begin identifying their emotions and develop their words to communicate in a healthy relationship. Don't force them to communicate. It will only push them away. It is not likely that they are even aware of their lack of connectedness.

Exercise

Communication is key to healing. Manners, respect, honesty, dependability, an ability to hear truth about blind spots and receive helpful criticism which requires emotional maturity. Making sure that you can resolve disagreements quickly, kindly and reconnect any break in the relationship takes genuine unselfish love and caring.

Application

Healthy Relationship Evaluation	
1.Not controlling or Manipulative	
2. Free to be you and develop your own identity, grow, and have your individuality.	
3. You can safely explore who you are.	
4. True love burns in your heart with a spiritual union that cannot be denied.	
5. You feel safe.	
6. You feel loved.	

7. You feel seen, heard, held, validated, assured.	
8. Your allowed to express all your scary inner parts: fear, anxiety, grief, depression, anger, grumpy, bully and your partner isn't afraid.	
9. You never go at each other… instead, you have healthy face to face conversations with truth and compassion.	
10. You never feel like you must lie or walk on eggshells.	
11. Trust is built from connectedness and excitement to be with each other.	
12. You allow the person to come and go. The love is secure… you know their heart is so connected they are coming back.	
13. You support them to make their own decisions.	
14. You are always for them and not against them.	
15. You hope the best, think the best, and are not accusatory.	
16. Forgive easily and reconnect quickly.	
17. Communication is easy.	
18. You can communicate without words.	
19. You never feel out of place, in the way or unwanted.	

21. You can feel their presence when they aren't there.	
22. You can't give or receive enough hugs and kisses.	
23. Emotional attunement is developed with giggles, noises, little growls, and eye contact. They are present when they are with you.	
24. They feel like your other half. You can't imagine life without them.	
26. You delight in them, and they delight in you.	
27. Sex is a gift to one another, not a chore. Your bodies belong to each other. Sex is not used as a weapon or for manipulation.	
28. You study the other one to find out what they like.	
29. You laugh a lot.	
30. You enjoy each other's company.	
31. Passion may eventually fail, but love endures.	
32. If your lonely, be vulnerable to one another.	
33. Be intentional with building relationship and community with others. Don't isolate as a couple.	

Today you are only allowed to have your own mood. Anyone who has an exaggerated negative emotion gets a hug. "Bring it in… let me give you a hug." Nothing is taken personal.

Skill Practice
1) Have your own mood and don't judge it, just acknowledge it, and let it pass.
2) Comfort others when they are unbalanced without taking it personal.

Principle

Healthy relationships are intentional.

Conclusion

Healthy relationships require give and take. Caring, sharing, and a building of friendship will grow. Accountability and open communication will be normal and not rare. Your boundaries will be respected. Your time will be valued. Trust, support, and shared power will be nurtured. One partner will not be condescending or talking down to the other.

Both partners will share equally with chore duties and child rearing. Conflicts will be easily resolved, and each partner will desire to correct themselves. A difference of opinions will be allowed. Manners will be practiced and both partners will apologize frequently and repair any relationship damage quickly.

Lord, help us make our homes a safe space. Give us joy and peace and the ability to communicate with each other with ease. Let us intentionally be safe for others to love and help us learn to enjoy our relationships. Amen

LESSON 2

TOXIC RELATIONSHIPS

People in toxic relationships give power away to gain power and control over another.

Introduction

If you give away your power to gain power and control over another, you lose your own identity! If you keep hooking into the same type of dysfunction, you need to work on healing your emotional nervous system that subconsciously is attracted to toxic individuals. You may be repeating your traumatic past to resolve it or find a better outcome. This causes you to inadvertently repeat the same type of harmful relationships.

> *Eventually your power and control are taken from you.*

Those in recovery have not developed a solid identity and are plagued with poor coping skills and emotional immaturity. There are also multiple unresolved childhood traumas, along with abandonment, neglect and a myriad of dysfunctional learned behaviors that need to be identified and unlearned.

These wounds make the luxury of casual sex or early recovery relationships deadly.

As we educate ourselves on what is healthy and what is toxic, we can learn self-awareness of our triggers and grow in the ability to self-regulate. We can develop a strong identity of ourselves and know what we want and need from a relationship. We will know our value and will not allow ourselves to be abused.

TOXIC RELATIONSHIP REVIEW

1. **Emotional dominance** - This abuser makes you second guess yourself. They twist words and pretend you are crazy. **They set you up to not even be able to trust yourself.** They play the victim to get sympathy. They tell you what you can or cannot think, say, or not say. You may frequently hear them say, "You shouldn't say that!"

Lesson

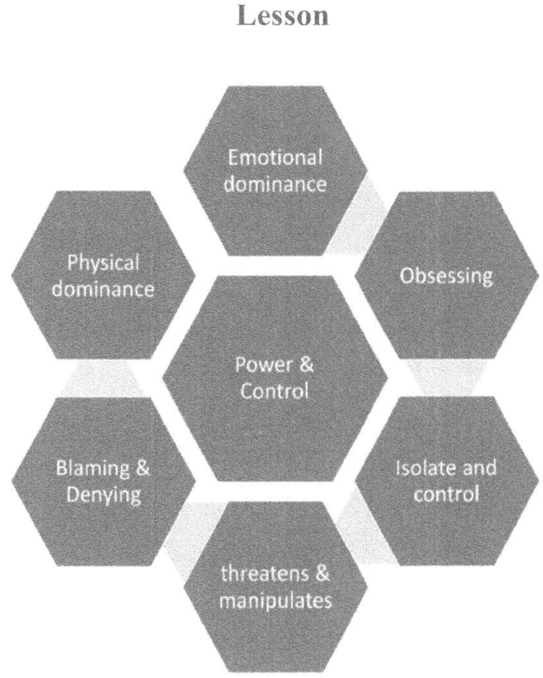

2. **Obsessing** over having their own way - Once the brain forms a negative loop of anxiety, fear, anger, or other intense emotion, it will obsess and repeat the pattern over and over. You know your loved one is obsessed if they are verbally tormenting you with repetitive loops. They may obsess about money, employers, neighbors, or even trivial things like the way the dish cloth is hung or how straight the shoes are lined up. The longer they obsess, the louder they vent. Their speech could be total lies, but eventually they will wear down their victim until the person gives in and agrees with them.

Disciplined thinking is greatly lacking. This building of offenses is intentional to justify their next substance use binge or your next beating.

3. **Isolating and controlling** - An abuser will slander and rail anyone in your life who could speak truth to you. They will separate and divide you from all healthy individuals. They use paranoia to control your thinking and alienate you from others. **If you are dating a person who dominates your thinking …run!**

4. **Threatens and manipulates -** A ranting, negative person uses anger to self-medicate. They use rage to release pent up emotions and self-regulate. You may react and fight back or may retreat and become passive and make excuses for the abuser. Either one is unnecessary in a healthy, trusting relationship. If you become your abuser's protector when natural consequences occur, (for example: domestic violence charges, assault & battery, arrest, relapse, etc.) you need more help than you can imagine. Go to a domestic violence shelter and ask about group counseling sessions. Go to counseling immediately.

5. **Blaming and Denying** – One in active addiction does not take responsibility for their actions. They are contentious with anyone who attempts to hold them accountable. Individuals with SUD (substance use disorder) will divide you and your loved ones or close friends and play you against each other to have power to continue in

their destructive behaviors without restraint. They will seek to build offenses against others and build negative bonds with empathetic sympathizers. This is a tactic to deflect personal responsibility for their actions and become a victim with enablers feeling sorry for them and making excuses for their poor decisions.

6. **Physical dominance -** This physical dominance and control is never love. It is using and abusing. If you walk on eggshells trying to keep the peace, don't! Disentangle yourself from this relationship until they understand and seek recovery for their dysfunctional personality issues.

> *Name calling the signature card of abuse.*
>
> *Blaming and playing the victim is the con game.*
>
> *An enabler is a master excuse maker.*
>
> *Stop making excuses for poor behavior and set up standards for your relationships.*

Exercise

Discuss toxic relationship warning signs.

Toxic Relationship Warning Signs	
1. Turns your words against you.	
2. Paranoid	
3. Makes villains out of those who disagree with them.	
4. Uses intimidation.	
5. "If you love me" manipulation statements.	
6. Threatens to hurt you or others.	
7. Threatens to hurt themselves.	
8. Road rage	
9. Escalates issues into a crisis when they do not get their way.	
10. Jealous	
11. Excessive texting, calling, emails, visits, etc.	
12. Insist you stop hanging out with other friends.	
13. Separates you from your family by being "offended" or causing an "offense".	

14. Controls where you go, what you wear, and what you do.	
15. Complaining and discontent	
16. Does not openly communicate problems.	
17. Refuses to resolve conflicts. Bears a grudge.	
18. Mood swings	
19. Disrespects authority	
20. Does not accept responsibility for their actions blames others.	
21. Frequently says:	
• You should not say that.	
• You interrupted me.	
• You do not know what you are saying.	
• You are stupid.	
• You are crazy.	
• You are not my teacher.	

Application

Helpless Syndrome aka total toxicity

Feeling helpless can paralyze you from deciding and:

- Keep you overwhelmed.
- Make you impulsive.
- Distract you from your goals.
- Allow you to deceive yourself for a little attention.
- Brings on depression.
- Make you want to use dysfunctional coping skills (addictive behaviors).
- Gives you insomnia, interrupts your sleep, anxiety and/or severe physical illness because of chronic fight or flight syndrome which causes **enervation** (loss of strength or vigor).

List for me what you will and will not tolerate in a relationship:

Decide

- What compromises are you willing to make to have a relationship?

- What price are you willing to pay to keep others from suffering their consequences for poor choices?

- What cost is too high?

Is it your health, safety, home, sanity, children, future security, stability, and/or your peace and quiet?

Is there an intense excitement alternating with a foreboding anxiety in this relationship?

> *A healthy relationship won't cause you anxiety.*

- What sacrifices have you made this past year to keep another comfortable?

  Was it worth the cost?

  Have they grown, changed, or regressed?

  Are you in a better position than a year ago?

- What would your future look like if you stayed in this relationship?

- What will it look like if you do not change?

- What would it look like if you withdrew your emotional, physical, or financial support?

- What are your greatest fears?

- What is the worst that could happen if you severe this relationship?

- What is the best thing that could happen?

Principle

People in toxic relationships give power away to gain power and control over another.

Conclusion

Relationship Toxicity

There are times in the past few years I have felt forsaken, forgotten, lost, and undone. Hearing the voice of reason, only to have circumstances prove me wrong. The confusion and torment have been greater, longer, and harder to overcome than I ever imagined. The fear, anxiety and frustration has been intermittently incomprehensible.

Even when, I find myself totally helpless. I always have choices, but sometimes no choice seems viable. So, my choice is to stay stuck in a cyclical pattern of abuse or choose to distance myself from the relationship and press onward and upward towards the peace I know can be mine.

The greatest skill I have learned is to not make decisions during times of confusion, but to stand still and stay the course until things become clear.

Sometimes, our relationships resemble our families. People take advantage of us and then control us, and this creates chaos that feels normal. We allow them to dominate our thinking and our entire life. We must emotionally set aside people that cause us suffering and make the best decision for ourselves. This takes courage and emotional maturity. This takes some stubborn resolve to protect our heart by closing it off to those who have proven themselves unsafe for us to freely trust and love.

When a person doesn't have their own identity and think we are like their right arm and can be moved and used as they see fit, they do not know how to respect another person's individuality. They weren't allowed to grow and mature as their own individual throughout childhood and are always insecurely attaching to others to find the part of themselves that didn't develop. Their interactions with others lack boundaries. Often, they are so empty inside that they lack the ability to see the effects of their behaviors on others.

Therefore, there is a skill we must develop where we toughen up and deafen our ears to manipulative emotional ploys. Does this sound cruel? It is much worse to continue rescuing than to allow others to face the consequences of their poor relational behaviors. This consequence is theirs, and not ours. If we assume responsibility for the electric bill when they just spent $100 eating out or smoking and vaping, we are keeping them from growing through overcoming their spending impulses through struggles of consequences.

If we continue to make excuses and rescue, others become dependent and will be angry as we disengage from them. This usually triggers an old abandonment wound and often causes relapse.

Do not engage in relationships in early recovery. Each person must form their own identity, inner strength and develop character to bounce back from disappointments. Otherwise, you keep circling the same mountain and land in the same place year after year. Forward movement and recovery progress will be continually hindered through repeating broken relationship patterns.

> *Who double-talks and usurps your decision-making skills?*

Most in recovery are greatly lacking in decision making skills.

Others know what decisions need to be made but **lack the resolve** to follow through with their choices. Still others know exactly what to do, until they are face to face with their current partner and then they become puppets and have absolutely no power. If you know what to do when you are alone or with a counselor and then cannot follow through with this in the presence of your toxic love, you need distance, space, and time to find yourself again. The voice of reason within you, has become the voice of confusion.

Lord, help me make healthy decisions. Guide me into healthy thinking and right living. Give me teachers that are patient with me. Give me ears to hear the instructions you have for me. Give me the courage to stop toxic relationships and seek my own inner health and well-being. Amen.

LESSON 3

RELATIONSHIP ADDICTION

If I am not content alone, I will never be content with another person.

Introduction

There is a difference between having an exciting lover and being able to be fully known and truly loved by another. If you are magnetically attracted to a person, it could be that you have activated a trauma bond. **Trauma Bond** is a feeling of magical connectedness. It feels familiar because it is like a dysfunctional dynamic in an earlier relationship. It most likely mirrors a childhood relationship with demanding, emotionally unavailable, or narcissistic parents. This familiar magical connection may suck you into toxic patterns of relating and repetitive patterns of dysfunction. You may interpret behaviors through distorted lenses of reality. The familiarity of the toxicity will feel like home.

Possibly you have regressed emotionally and feel compelled to ignore all the red flags and let this relationship play out. Or it could be that you are an object to be controlled and are naïve and simply being reeled in.

Maybe you have something the person needs or desires. Maybe you just came out of a toxic relationship and the love bombing with this new person is comforting and you don't recognize the addictive relationship patterns.

Lesson

Love Bombing is intense, overwhelming, exaggerated affection at the beginning of a relationship. This can look and feel like the normal honeymoon phase in a healthy relationship. Time will tell if this is the beginning of a relationship addiction cycle or even the ploy of a groomer who is attempting to extort you for gain. It could be a narcissistic player needing to get their emotional high met with the hunt and chase of a new relationship but have no clue how to develop a healthy relationship. Think slow, time, distance, space, and not sexual intimacy for months. You will thank me later.

After the **honeymoon phase** of a relationship, it will be characterized by steady growth and maturity. Unity and connectedness will develop with mutual respect and dependability. The couple will develop common goals. This is healthy.

But, if this is a **relationship addiction**, there will be anxiety, confusion and difficulty regulating emotions. It may be a push-pull relationship with lots of red flags. But the love bombing may be blocking your intuition like clouds can block the sun. If you have previously been ignored and rejected in close relationships, this type of attention can feel validating and supportive. The constant attention or excessive texting feels pleasant and not obsessive or controlling. By the time you figure out this relationship has toxic qualities, if you let it move too fast, you may be stuck.

When you are stuck emotionally in a toxic relationship, the confusion is high. You have been groomed to not trust your instincts. As soon as you see a trait as potentially lethal to the relationship and acknowledge it openly, the love bombing will reemerge.

Although the intense attentiveness re-emerges it will never be as intoxicating as it was at the beginning when you were the center of the universe. The previous love bombing was so pleasant you may be willing to settle for crumbs waiting on the romantic intensity to return. This phase is the addictive lure of the relationship that keeps you on the hook.

You speak about magical connection and how blessed you are to have found the fairytale when the relationship begins. In a toxic relationship when the love bombing phase diminishes, you are on the hook. Your happiness is being controlled depending upon your conformity to your new identity that is being shaped.

You don't understand your identity is being torn down and reshaped through a technique called *gaslighting.* Gaslighting is part of the grooming process. *It denies your reality and breaks your identity and mentally reshapes you into thinking you are crazy*. If you fight back, you are facing a bully and confused. You begin to assume responsibility for their emotional stability. Next, they are a wounded victim that triggers the nurturer in you.

Soon you are managing their emotions and propping them up from their despair. You are the new savior. What would they do without you? Emotionally you start to become so focused on this person, that you completely lose your goals and direction in life. Most likely you have previously formed a *fake self* and don't have a strong identity. A person with a strong identity will exit this unstable relationship quickly.

A person who never fully formed their own identity will stay just to see where this goes. The roller coaster of a toxic relationship is addictive. If you grew up in a home with exaggerated high and low emotions, this feels normal.

Pseudo loyalty to the other will demand you stay. *A healthy person will know this is toxic loyalty that requires you to abandon your own self. This is not loyalty at all but self-abandonment characteristic of an enabling rescuer.* It is like loyalty to a poisonous snake that will bite you. Healthy self-love will want emotional stability in a partner who cherishes them as an individual and doesn't try to dominate or control them.

Toxic partners begin to reshape your thinking and tell you who you are and what you will and will not do. The next moves are possessive and sharing. But it is them, possessing your property and you sharing everything. Everything belongs to them. You're not likely allowed to have your own emotions and are required to drop everything at a moment's notice. You will even be called selfish or other derogatory names if you establish a boundary. This is another manipulative, bullying, gaslighting tactic.

The root of this issue is that they do not have their own identity and are developing it within the relationship with you. Their ways are moveable. They don't even know who they are or what they think.

Any "no" may be challenged. If you persist with a boundary, it is likely you will be called cruel, mean, and uncaring. Sometimes if they need something they will ask nicely, other times they will just take it. They attempt to make themselves indispensable in your life. They tell you that they need you to survive, and you need them. They start making decisions for you, after all, they know what is best for you.

Enmeshment begins early, they become thoroughly entrenched in your life. Boundaries are pushed through, with your permission of course. After a flipping of words mixed with charm or pouting, you have no clue which way is up or down. *Disentangling from this person will be messy and may take an act of congress.*

Your superpower will be placing firm boundaries and standing your ground. Once you are not an easy mark, not stroking their ego or making excuses for them, they will quickly go for easier prey. If you have any doubt, step back for six months, you will find you are wrong, and this could be a safe, strong, dependable relationship and a strong friendship has developed. Or you will find they got over you pretty darn quick and moved on.

Exercise

Relationship Addiction Evaluation	
1. Feels magical and connected.	
2. Feels like the fairytale with lots of attention and love-bombing.	
3. Your fantasy thoughts of a healthy relationship are clouding your judgment of the real relationship.	
4. You are powerfully attracted to this person.	
5. You both obsess over each other.	
6. You feel cherished. (The reality is you are being controlled.)	
7. You feel protected. (Reality is you are trapped with constant attention.)	
8. Your friends are being devalued.	
9. Offenses are being set up between you and protectors.	
10. Your friends warn you of red flags.	

11. You can't follow through with your own decisions when you are with them.	
12. You break up and go back often.	

Stuck	
1. Euphoric recall of past love-bombing.	
2. Romanticizing the good and forgetting the bad.	
3. Unable to follow through with any decision.	
4. They start making decisions for you.	
5. Loss of your own identity.	
6. Loss of self-control. You can be moved like a puppet.	
7. Roller coaster emotions.	
8. Push-pull behaviors. Come here… go away.	
9. Fear of letting go.	
10. Overly focused on pleasing the other to the point of walking on eggshells and lots of compromises to appease the other.	
11. Your opinions will be reshaped.	
12. You are powerless to leave.	
13. Staying for crumbs of attention waiting for the love-bombing to return.	
14. You hear yourself making a lot of excuses. This is called *gaslighting yourself.* They have been shifting your reality and it is difficult to clearly see the truth. Everything is confusing. Your anxiety is high and	

difficult to manage. Often you are paralyzed to make any decision. You want to leave. Wait! You want to stay.	

Application

Escape the Relationship Addiction Cycle
1. Heal your inner self.
2. Know what you want in a partner.
3. Know what you will and will not tolerate.
4. Understanding relationship addiction patterns.
5. Have strong healthy boundaries.
6. Say no often. Build your own identity.
7. Push back on any dominance.
8. Correct any immature victim mentality on both sides.
9. Accept responsibility for your actions.
10. Don't make yourself too available.
11. Don't answer texts quickly and see if the person has a meltdown or if they are disrespectful of your time.
12. Voice your opinions and see if they are respected or reshaped.
13. Be slow to make decisions.

Principle

If I am not content alone, I will never be content with another person.

Application

If you work on your healing, you will likely be too much work and one with the motive of a player will move on. If they are in 3-4 relationships a year, they are toxic and addicted to the chase. If they always cheated on their past partners, they may like the stability of a solid relationship but get bored and need outside sources of attention to supply their ego.

They may experience no remorse and have no conscience awareness of how they are hurting their partner. Also, a person with trauma is usually restless and struggles to settles down.

If they have already started having an affair, instead of breaking up with their partner in a responsible manner, they may become offended over trivial things and be irritable. This is a *chess move of blame shifting*. That way if they are caught, well, you made them unhappy in the relationship and they can blame you. It was your fault for not paying attention to them.

Conclusion

In relationships just as in scuba diving you can get confused and not know which way is up or down. The advice of a scuba instructor is not to panic but to sit still and soon you will see which way the bubbles are going. Bubbles always float up. Then you will know which direction to go for safety. So, in relationships if you are confused, sit still. Don't make any quick decisions. Calm your anxiety or even your need to be in this relationship and sit quietly, you will soon know which way is up.

If you have escaped a toxic relationship and are now grieving the love bombing stage, it is a nice memory. That is called *euphoric recall.* Beware as time passes, you may forget the bad and only remember the good. That is called *romanticizing the past.*

Instead, make a trouble list. Write out all the toxic behaviors.

Give the confusion and anxiety of the relationship a toxicity level between 1-10.

One being very low and near normal to 10 being in fear of your life and volatile anger and domestic violence. Often escaping these relationships makes you feel stabbed in the back or leave your heart sliced open. You will be forever changed.

This will make you wiser or drive you back to the toxicity of relationship addiction patterns to develop enabler/rescuer behaviors and repeat this cycle multiple times throughout your lifespan. These relationships are very difficult to end. This is **relationship addiction.**

Lord, help me to recognize your voice. Help me discern good from evil, right from wrong, healthy from toxic. Help me to be content alone and to be able to sit quietly in your presence and let you fill me with your presence. Give me the strength and courage and understanding to protect my heart with all diligence. I love you, Jesus.

LESSON 4

CODEPENDENCY

Healthy relationships require emotional fitness.

Introduction

When I have broken down pillars in my life, I choose broken people. I may choose people with more problems than myself. This way I do not have to focus working on me. I can focus on the struggles and the problems of another person.

In codependency, my empathic radar is in full force. A strong empath muscle develops in childhood. Possibly I parented my parents. Possibly I was their comforter. This rescuer mentality is my identity. Then passivity keeps the boat from being rocked and keeps others from targeting me and I make myself very small, almost invisible. This type of submission will **attract** the insecure attachment of dominance and controlling. A controlling person is insecure in who they are and needs an object of control.

Codependency Evaluation?	
1) Am I a giver or a taker?	
2) Do I attract dominate or passive people?	
3) How many times have I lived with someone or been divorced?	
4) Can I break up with another person maturely without blaming them and creating drama?	
5) Will I stay in a relationship that isn't suited to me?	
6) Do I stay to avoid hurting someone else's feelings?	
7) Do I have healthy co-parenting relationships with ex-partners?	
8) Do I entertain depression often?	
9) Do I meddle in other people's problems?	
10) Am I a fixer? A pleaser?	
11) Can I turn off my affections quickly when I recognize I am being used or abused?	
12) Do I have a good support team?	
13) Can I ask my support team to evaluate a new potential partner and follow their advice?	

14) Have I done the work to heal from past hurts and wounds?	
15) Do I have healthy and peaceful contentment with myself?	
16) Have I made movement in the last year or am I stuck in negative rumination over past toxicity?	

Personal Boundaries are clear directions for how we allow people to treat us.

The first step to conquering codependency is to have strong boundaries. Sit down with a trusted friend and decide what boundaries are lacking in your life and where you need more.

Time Boundaries	Physical Boundaries	Conversation
• How much time will you spend with someone? • How much time do you schedule on an activity?	• Boundaries around physical proximity, sexuality, & how much space you share with others.	• Boundaries what topics are you open to discussing or not discussing and with whom?

• How are your boundaries at work? • Can you say “no”?		• Do I need boundaries with my words? • No complaining • No arguing • No slandering or gossip.
<u>Relationship Boundaries</u> • What boundaries mutually agreed upon with your close friends and partner do you need?	<u>Personal Boundaries</u> • Boundaries you have placed with yourself based on awareness of your own unique needs.	<u>Content Boundaries</u> • Things you will and will not consume or will have accountability like social media, TV, etc.

When will you block someone from your social media? When will you block someone from your phone contacts? Are others allowed to call you with a crisis in the middle of the night? Are others allowed to make their problems your problems. Learn to recognize when you are in a sick syndrome that will make you vulnerable. After you have helped someone for a certain amount of time and they are worse, back off from the relationship. If you try to help others and they sabotage themselves and then blame you, distance yourself for a while.

Sick Syndrome

Here are some personal growth points to journal about and work through with a trusted friend. We often have blind spots and repeat patterns that others can see, but we cannot.

1. Do I lack love for myself?

2. Do I lack understanding of who I am?
3. Is my desire to be fulfilled with a relationship too strong?
4. Am I a pleaser?
5. Do I rescue and enable others to stay sick?
6. Am I a fantasizer with a fairytale mentality?
7. Am I needy, unfulfilled, wounded?

These struggles will develop vulnerability without direction within a person.

Application

Watch the birds, they build a nest together. This is teamwork. The one searches and provides for food while the other keeps the eggs warm. *This is interdependency*. When a predator is seen, the colorful male will fly a distance away and cry to get the attention of the predator who would rob the nest. *This is protection.* The one will sacrifice himself to protect his mate and the nest of unhatched eggs.

When the eggs hatch, they stay close and work fervently to feed the hatchlings. *This is a duty, commitment and nurturing* the chicks together. When the babies are ready, there is a *launching and letting go.* There may even be a pushing out of the nest. Then a training of the chicks to find their own food. *This is releasing adult children.*

Love is teamwork, interdependency, protection, sacrifice, staying close and meeting the needs of each other, commitment, nurturing, launching, and letting go. Birds fly away and come back to their nest. They know instinctively where the nest is and where they belong. Your family may not have done this for you. It may be that you need to empower your adult self to do this for you.

Principle

Healthy relationships require emotional fitness.

Conclusion

Do I often get scared and abandon others at the beginning of a relationship, or do I give it a chance? This may be an attachment wound like *anxious avoidance* that needs healed. True relationships require vulnerability and trust.

When I find a person who can defend and protect my honor, I am safe to love in return. Toxic and healthy relationships often start the same way. It is important to develop all romantic relationships slowly. Start with friendship and observing them in a group or family setting.

If you have experienced abuse or any other form of violence, you will become a different person. This may make you more vulnerable to other toxicity. This may develop unhealthy obsessive *limerence which is repetitive romantical thoughts of another*. This unhealthy ruminating over a person can bond you with your imaginary lover, not the real person. This behavior is addictive and confusing and will keep you stuck and returning to a toxic relationship. *Limerence focuses your attention on the other person, and you lose your own ability to move on after this relationship.* This behavior will need counseling and supportive groups or friendships to heal.

Instead, I want you to grow stronger and learn to believe in yourself. May you become your best defender. May you learn to be safe in your own skin and enjoy a peaceful heart. May you learn to sit with your anxiety until you find a river of peace flowing within.

Oh Lord, relationships are difficult to sustain. Will you help me to develop strength and health in relationships? Help me to develop a healthy sense of myself. Help me to know where I begin and where I end. Let me love intelligently by seeing clearly and choosing what is best for my future. First, I choose you. O Lord, be my first love and help me to heal and feel loved by you. Amen.

LESSON 5

RELATIONSHIP BONDAGE

Perversion of truth is manipulation.

Introduction

Selfishness perverts' relationships by establishing demands, usurping authority, and taking control over another's life. This is a *relational captivity plot* with a goal of total bondage. They cannot maintain a healthy relationship. They will not listen or value your needs. They will dominate until you have no identity. It doesn't start out this way, your capture listens to all your hurts and hang-ups to get to know how to manipulate you. They study to know where you are weak and vulnerable. They know exactly what you need to hear them say. They may think they have found a healthy relationship but are incapable of maintaining it, because of their own unresolved addictive patterns.

The game locks you into a toxic relationship and you feel powerless to escape. You may see Red Flags and yet are powerless to act to protect yourself. You must betray yourself to participate in a toxic relationship. *Self-betrayal entertains toxicity and becomes captive to rescuing another and keeps you stuck.* If you want healthy relationships, educate yourself on the toxic dynamics of abusive relationships and fight to heal and be free of toxicity.

Self-Betrayal is foundational to entertaining a toxic relationship.

Lesson

1) **There are people who pervert truth to their own advantage, and they are good at it. Reject their nonsense.**

Paul says, (2) *I am jealous for you with a godly jealousy. I promised you to one husband, to Christ, so that I might present you as a pure virgin to him. (3) But I am afraid that just as Eve was deceived by the serpent's cunning, your minds may somehow be led astray from your sincere and pure devotion to Christ. (4) For if someone comes to you and preaches a Jesus other than the Jesus we preached, or if you receive a different spirit from the one you received, or a different gospel from the one you accepted, you put up with it easily enough. 2 Corinthians 11:2-4*

2) **Deceitful people can be so convincing because they have even deceived themselves. Recognize the lies.**

Paul says, (13) For such men are false apostles, deceitful workmen, masquerading as apostles of Christ. (14) And no wonder, for Satan himself masquerades as an angel of light. (15) It is not surprising, then, if his servants masquerade as servants of righteousness. 2 Corinthians 11:13-15

Rebellion develops a trap.

Often, individuals with abusive behaviors can pretend to be extremely kind. But say, "no" to them and see if they respect your "no" or if they flip personalities and become depraved and incorrigible. If so, the "real" person beneath the cloak of pretense has just been unveiled.

Exercise

Captivity Evaluation	
1) Am I being charmed and corrupted away from stability?	
You gladly put up with fools since you are so wise! In fact,	

you even put up with anyone who enslaves you or exploits you or takes advantage of you or pushes himself forward or slaps you in the face. 2 Corinthians 11:19-20	
2) Are they pretending that everything they do is right and refusing counsel?	
3) Has my peace been devoured?	
4) Has my freedom been hampered?	
5) Do they run recklessly down the road with no thought of the consequences?	
6) Are they taking my money, time, and energy?	
7) Am I assuming their responsibilities?	
8) If I confront them, do they hit me physically or bully me with words or double talk using gas lighting techniques or do they listen and change?	

Handling Truth Perverters.

In trying to please the unpleasable people in my life, I have forgotten to be true to myself.

Am I trying to win the approval of men, or of God? Or am I trying to please men? If I were still trying to please men, I would not be a servant of Christ. Galatians 1:10

Think of this perverter as the television, an inanimate object that can speak but not hear. They control you with manipulative, fearful, or bullying tactics through indoctrination of their philosophies. These people twist truth and coerce you with fear. They could be in your schools, communities, churches, or even in your home. They speak their great swelling words over and over until they believe their own lies and bully others until they shut up and go along with them.

Those that use perversion of truth are masters at manipulation.

(6) I am astonished that you are so quickly deserting the one who called you by the grace of Christ and are turning to a different gospel— (7) which is really no gospel at all. Evidently some people are throwing you into confusion and are trying to pervert the gospel of Christ. (8) But even if we or an angel from heaven should preach a gospel other than the one, we preached to you, let him be eternally condemned! Galatians 1:6-8

We cannot find balance in chaos. Turn off the chaos. Get alone, journal, get quiet, and find your own way. In cases of recovery, many return to an old dysfunctional relationship, and are shoved into the path of a speeding train of destruction. After several recovery attempts… you have only one viable choice, **save yourself and let people go with abusive, manipulative, rebellious, dominate**

people who you cannot save.

...how is it that you are turning back to those weak and miserable principles? Do you wish to be enslaved by them all over again? Galatians 4:9b

Look past the passion and flattery. Demand evidence of genuine heart change. Others do not need to change if we are continually zealous to make excuses for them. Your courage to say no to them may be their only hope.

Paul says, (17) Those people are zealous to win you over, but for no good. What they want is to alienate you from us (recovery), so that you may be zealous for them. (18) It is fine to be zealous, provided the purpose is good, and to be so always and not just when I am with you. Galatians 4:17-18

Ask yourself:

- Who am I trying to please?
- Am I addicted to a person and think of them constantly?
- Do I hear myself rationalizing with an irrational person and having the same conversation over and over?
- Have I been bewitched (controlled), entangled, or enticed? *You foolish Galatians!*

Who has bewitched you? ... Are You so foolish? After beginning with the Spirit, are you now trying to attain your goal by human effort? Galatians 3:1

- Am I focused on trying to fix someone else?
- Do I think money is all I need to solve problems?

When we have freed ourselves, <u>do not</u> forget the chronic days, weeks, and years of abuse. Do not turn away from freedom and go back into the cycle of abuse! The key is to get free and stay free. Hide yourself. Run!

Relationship addiction is a bondage that needs the work of sobriety as if your life depends upon it.

It is for freedom that Christ has set us free. Stand firm, then, and do not let yourselves be burdened again by the yoke of slavery. Galatians 5:1

Application

Burden Evaluation
1) How have people with addictive or abusive behaviors

affected me?
2) What burdens have others put on me?
3) What burdens have I accepted and put on myself that wasn't mine?

4) How has my daily peace been hindered?
5) Do I have a *repetition compulsion* and end up in the same type of relationships repeatedly? Different face, different name, different place, but the exact same scenarios of dominance and abuse.
Truth: Those causing trouble need to bear their own consequences (and they should). When I set up boundaries and am no longer accessible to be manipulated, they will change or have no use for me and leave me alone.

Truth:

If I don't do my healing work, I will end up in the exact same type of relationship with an emotionally unavailable person with various sick behaviors.

Words are powerless, demand the voice of action!

*** When we use our **NO muscle** and others separate themselves from us, it's okay!

Paul says, (7) You were running a good race. Who cut in on you and kept you from obeying the truth? (8) That kind of persuasion does not come from the one who calls you…(10a) I am confident in the Lord that you will take no other view… (12) As for those agitators, I wish they would go the whole way and emasculate (cut themselves off from you) themselves! Galatians 5:7,8,10a,12

This separating or "cutting off" usually comes with great drama when we are placing healthy boundaries. Expect it. **Die (detach) emotionally to a sick relationship,** so we cannot be emotionally manipulated. They will return as a victim when their next lover (enabler) turns them out or when they think you have softened, and they can return to get their needs met.

Make them **earn the right** to be trusted by showing a good work ethic and making restitutions for their wrongs. Do not just accept words of apology or a "hard luck" story. Most people are incapable of change. The blessing of recovery is *internal reflection* and the journaling to develop our own *self-awareness*.

The realization that I can only work on me, and I must release others and trust that they can find their own way has given me incredible peace. Anxiety is a signal that I have recovery work to do.

Remember the law of sowing and reaping. *Do not be deceived: God cannot be mocked. A man reaps what he sows. The one who sows to please his sinful nature, from that nature will reap destruction; the one who sows to please the Spirit, from the Spirit will reap eternal life. Galatians 6:7-8*

We sow to the wind and reap the whirlwind. Hosea 8:7

Do not stick your head in the sand and think problems will go away. Instead, work on things that are within your control to change. You can only change you!

Hold onto your freedom to regain control over your own life. Do not get entangled again. **Hold your head high and speak no unkind words.** Turn and walk away from filth, don't even honor it with an answer. **Stick to your beliefs in the simplicity of hard work and responsibility.**

...we gave you this rule: "If a man will not work, he shall not eat." 2 Thessalonians 3:10

So, do you recognize those with impure motives?

Do you love a person who refuses to take responsibility for their actions?

It may take a few weeks or months but develop a plan to thoughtfully untangle yourself and create distance until they pursue being responsible.

Who is hindering you and keeping you emotionally unstable?

Are you hindering another? Go and apologize quickly.

Principle

Perversion of truth is manipulation.

Conclusion

Now to you who are suffering from the emotional pain of abuse, I apologize. I am truly sorry for your suffering. I apologize to you for everyone who has ever hurt you and are unable or unwilling to repent. I give you permission to release your offender from the debt they owe you. I set you free.

Take a deep breath and exhale and let go. This is a new day. May you be free to be the person you were created to be. May you be internally like steel, unmovable and unshakeable.

Lord God, grant me a place of internal peace. Help me to guard my peace from those who pervert the truth and rob me of the right to have a quiet life. Help me to discern those with impure motives and to hide myself from them. Make me mighty in spirit: unmovable and unshakeable. Give me strength to recognize and refuse manipulation. Amen.

LESSON 6

TRAUMA BONDING

Obsession is magnetically strong

but is not love.

Introduction

Make relationship decisions very slowly. Weather at least four seasons and a couple crises with a person before making a commitment. Study yourself and work on your weaknesses. Work on your emotional wounds. Don't compare your journey to someone else's.

Stop judging your emotions and thoughts. Just identify them. Be gracious and learn to love yourself in a healthy and sanctified way. When we give from a wounded place of emptiness, relationship stability is hard to find, and we tend to be triggered and repeat old wounds in new relationships.

Instead, we must nurture ourselves in a healthy, sanctified way to heal and develop a healthy identity. This is not selfish; it is the development of a sanctified self. A *sanctified self* remembers to do what is best for me and my future, has strong boundaries and nurtures myself with self-care every day. A sanctified self has inner peace and speaks kindly to oneself and extends grace to weaker, broken parts of myself and never judges or condemns.

Lesson

If you are love starved, anyone that pays attention to you can look like a viable partner. Attentiveness from another can fill that internal void. Especially if the person is intense and mirroring your needs through nurturing and validation that you may not have received in a long time, if ever.

Then sometimes the flirtatious energy is so strong that you can make a hundred excuses for the obvious red flags. This energy makes an internal broken or dead part of you come alive. You may find a piece of yourself that was hidden shut down or you didn't know existed. If you are obsessing over a person and it is not likely to end well for either of you. This means you are attempting to find your authentic identity in another. This isn't possible.

LOVE STARVED

1) Anything that remotely looks like love, we gorge on if we are starving. This can end in destruction with relapse and even death.

2) When your heart is starving, it is nearly impossible to love, all responses become selfish. Feed your heart on the love of God. Be led into his steadfast love so you have an inner flow that is vibrant and giving. Otherwise, it is difficult to receive or sustain love, you can only consume it and be left more broken.

3) There is a difference between loving to get your needs met and loving others for their value. When you know your value, you can love even the unlovable and radically accept them with strong boundaries and without expectations for them to change.

When I am a broken person, I may settle for *crumbs*. I may lower my standards. I may know I am going into a toxic relationship, make a thousand excuses, and see multiple red flags and not be able to stop myself. My friends may be warning me and yet I am making every excuse because I am *love starved.* These relationships start too fast and develop toxicity quickly.

The key is to learn that all you need is within you. As a child, you needed others to protect and provide for you. As an adult your identity may not be solid. You may be looking for others to complete you and meet your needs and this keeps you *hyper focused* on controlling or consuming others and not on a relaxed, flowing, gentle easier healthy relationships.

Do you consistently choose others that are broken and try to fix them? Instead, turn your focus inward and work on yourself.

TRAUMA BONDING

Trauma bonding is a familiar vibrational pull back into toxicity that resembles your home of origin or past broken relationships. It has been suggested that we repeat these patterns attempting to resolve old relationship wounds or perhaps because they feel familiar.

Intense attraction may only be an old trauma bond. I must wait until physical attraction resolves itself. I can talk about it to a trusted friend. I can recognize this person likely isn't spiritually or emotionally healthy but is vibrationally connected to me through some past trauma that resembles mine. I can write out my red flag lists.

Adults of childhood abuse think with feelings and not with cognitive reasoning.

If you have a string of broken relationships, gravitate repeatedly to toxicity, or been trapped in domestic violence multiple times, do not have a relationship until you work on strengthening your inner self. This usually takes a year or two of solid work.

Exercise

Red Flag Evaluation	
1) Are they on the rebound from a disastrous relationship?	
2) Are they in a toxic relationship they are struggling to end?	
3) Do they lie often?	
4) Are they obsessing over you?	
5) Are you obsessing over them?	
6) Are they confessing their attraction as intense sexual desire?	
7) Do they have a history of being unfaithful?	
8) How many times have they been divorced or ended a long-term relationship? Was it amicable or volatile?	
9) Have they owned their part in past relationship failures, or do they play the victim?	
10) Have they done the work emotionally to heal from past relationships?	
11) Are they emotionally healthy enough to start a new relationship?	
12) Do they have strong mood swings?	
13) What are their family relationships like?	
14) Do you hear yourself making excuses for them?	

15) Does their walk match their talk?	
16) Are they respectful of your boundaries?	
17) Can they *self-regulate* and find inner peace quickly without indulging strong intense emotions?	

Toxic Relationship Vulnerability	
1) Wounded heart	
2) Past rejection and broken relationships	
3) Unfulfilled desire to be loved	
4) Unmet emotional, physical needs	
5) Unstable identity	
6) Looking to another person for completeness	
7) Too kind and empathetic	
Childhood neglect, abuse, abandonment, or trauma	

Identifying More Red Flags	
1) Lustful and/or obsessive	
2) Super-fast and intense connection	
3) Double-minded with push-pull tendencies	
4) Confusion or anxiety	
5) Regressing emotionally after initial few days/weeks of love bombing: lying, manipulation, control, dominance, ungrateful, or entitled.	
6) Emotionally charged highs and lows	

7) Repetitive past relationship failures with toxic breakups.	
8) Blame shifting, victim thinking, then bully behaviors.	
9) Overly concerned about what people think.	
10) Unresolved bitterness from any past relationship	

Application

Take your time in a new relationship. Make sure you aren't making yourself available just because you're lonely. Make sure you are emotionally healthy enough to start a new relationship without losing your own self. Make certain this is an emotionally available person. Let the relationship grow and develop slowly. It takes time to determine if it is lust or a healthy attraction.

Intense attentiveness may feel reassuring
but could be the beginning of toxic control.

Rules of Engagement	
1) Do not get entangled financially in a relationship for at least two years.	
2) Don't give away your financial power or independence…ever.	
3) Weather four seasons and a couple crises with a person before making a long-term commitment.	

4) Discern a person's entitlement and gratitude level.	
5) Complainers rarely make good partners.	
6) Angry people are hard to please.	
7) Discern their work ethic. Can they keep a job?	
8) Are they naturally a giver or a taker?	
9) Unless they are a good con; a person's speech will eventually detail their intentions and motives.	
10) Move slowly to intimate levels. A player will get bored and move on if they are only looking for quick ego supply.	

Principle

Obsession is magnetically strong but is not love.

Conclusion

Fighting may be the stronger side of yourself protecting your weaker self. Standing your ground and building strong boundaries is healthy. If someone pushes until they break your boundaries and you tiptoe, make excuses, and stop fighting back you're in danger of losing your own identity and becoming helpless and stuck in toxicity.

Let your yes be yes and your no be no. *…but let your yea be yea; and your nay, nay; lest you fall into condemnation. James 5:12 (KJV)*

When you see red flags don't make excuses, step back and let things unfold. Healthy relationships build trust bonds over time and are not in a hurry. **Toxic relationships move fast and trap you quickly. Slow down**! See the snare coming and hide. *The prudent see danger and take refuge, but the simple keep going and pay the penalty. Proverbs 27:12*

Lord, help me to recognize red flags and danger signs and refuse to make excuses. Give me the ability to trust my intuition. Help me to heal and prepare for healthy relationships. Help me to identify toxicity and repent quickly and give me the power to change my thinking and behaviors. Amen.

LESSON 7

RELATIONSHIP ADDICTION CYCLE

Relationship addictions suck the life out of you.

Introduction

This lesson is for those who want free from a relationship addiction. You must recognize the cycle of a dysfunctional relationship or will end up in the same place repeatedly unless you resist the cycle and develop your own thinking. Anytime you meet someone and there is intense attraction distance yourself until you have observed their behavior and investigated their past relationship history with others. If you have healthy boundaries, you will not give in to the impulse to follow this attraction. Set your standards higher and develop strong boundaries.

This cycle is different from trauma bonding. Trauma bonding can have two broken people clinging to one another. They have developed *fear bonds* from their past and have *insecure attachments* to overcome. **One or both people will build their identity in the other person and work on controlling the other person, but they lose themselves and their ability to grow and move forward in life in the process.**

In a relationship addiction cycle it is beyond control. It may have started with a trauma bond but now escalated to an addictive level. It is a devouring of another person for the thrill of the hunt or chase. The relationship phases are cyclical and can be observed. These relationships are not mature adults with good character. They cannot develop in a healthy manner. One or both partners can have narcissistic traits and be incapable of loving another. The relationship can be very volatile.

Educating yourself in these patterns will help you to do what is best for yourself and to break free quicker and with less emotional victimization. You can stand up and guard yourself and exercise your *no muscle* when you recognize the patterns. *A good "no" muscle develops strong healthy boundaries to protect yourself.*

A devouring relationship is not likely one that will ever be healthy. If you are in a marriage like this, you can stay or go. But the only way you can survive if you stay is to allow yourself the ability to grow and *radically accept* that this person will not or cannot change. Do not expect them to become someone different, they aren't capable. Accept them the way they are or move on. It's the only sane thing to do.

These patterns are usually romantic relationships. But dynamics of these patterns can be seen in work environments and with parents or siblings. This person may or may not have a history of mental illness.

Lesson

Intense Passion: Addicted to Love
• A consuming and exciting relationship
• You become the center of the world.
• Feel valued and loved and needed.
• Lots of affection and intensity
• You become the answer to their emptiness.
• Love Bombing aka emotional manipulation. This can be real. It can feel like real love. But it is impossible to sustain long term and the next step in the cycle will ensue.

Reality: You are their *latest obsession*. They are in love with the idea of being in love, but not with you.

- Appearances are important.

- Lust is strong; it feels like devotion and true love.
- They are intensely gratified with you.
- You are set up as their *savior.*
- This is the answer to their chasm of emptiness.
- Long talks
- Multiple daily texts and/or calls
- Your time is being consumed.
- Other relationships are pushed aside.
- You start to **lose your identity** and are molded into a new one.

Potential Pitfalls
• Emotionally unavailable (trust issues)
• Unhappily Married (need new source of ego supply)
• Rebound (consumed with grief)
• Man-eater (playful and alluring)
• Womanizer (addicted to the chase)
• Early recovery (lots of instability)
• Friends with benefits (commitment issues)
• Shirking duties (looking for enabler)

4 PHASES OF THE DEVOURING

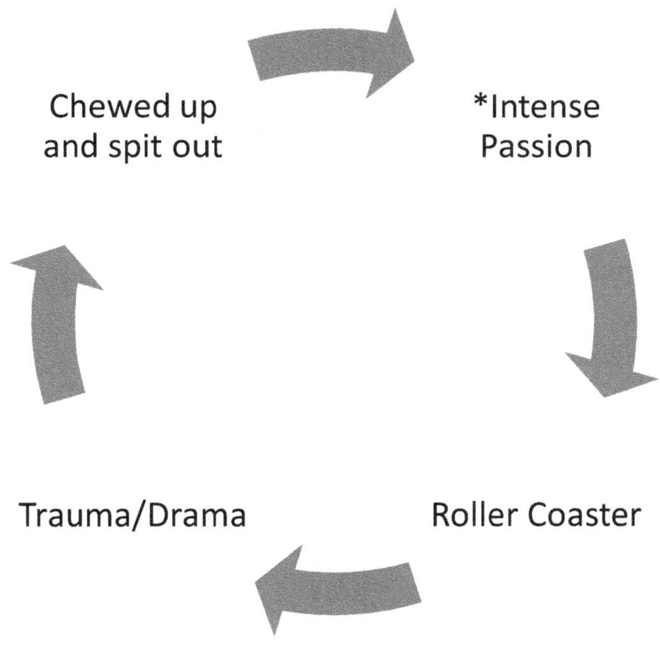

Roller Coaster (Manipulation Begins)

- Discontent sets in
- Mood swings
- His/her ways are moveable.
- You feel like you are trying to hold the wind.
- Whatever pleased them yesterday angers them today.

- Intense emotional highs/lows
- You begin the role of the "pleaser".
- Loss of your identity and you are remolded into a *fake self.*
- Your responsibility is to make them happy.
- Keeping them emotionally stable is a full-time job.
- Their eyes are at the end of the world.

    1. I want…
    2. Give me…
    3. If you really cared… A shower of satisfaction and gratefulness comes when they achieve what they want. Until they want the next thing…
    4. Cycle repeats (it usually intensifies… demands are greater)
    5. Usually there is a new hoop to jump through every day or even every hour.
    6. Whether they rage or laugh there is no peace. *If a wise man contends with a foolish man, whether he rage or laugh, there is no rest. Proverbs 29:9 (KJV)*
    7. The nagging and whining returns (Discontent)
    8. I want…

9. I need…
10. Only if…
11. A continual replay of old wounds…
12. And disappointments of old relationships rehashed….
13. The agitation begins verbally and mounts until they can justify their position… sometimes the position is an act of violence/theft (cleaning out your bank account) or other violation towards you. Recognize the cycle.

The leech has two daughters. "Give! Give!" They cry. Proverbs 30:15

Trauma/Drama – The Game Heats Up

1. Eventually, no matter what you do, it is not good enough.
2. Pushing buttons.
3. Unreasonable demands.
4. Just to see if you will play the *love game*, because of course any boundary or "no" is evil and **not** respected.
5. Comparison is made to an imaginary perfect relationship.
6. Turning your words against you.
7. Bringing up your past.
8. Self-pity, tears.

9. Depression.
10. Intense anger in them and/or in you.
11. Quick mood swings.

> *If your identity is wrapped up in another,*
> *you will feel responsible to make them happy.*

Chewed up and Spit Out

1. Confusion
2. Blaming
3. Name calling
4. Withdraw
5. Silent treatment
6. Obsessing
7. Slandering
8. They live in fantasy and not reality. Pornography is common. Obsessing is normal.
9. Then, there is shame, guilt or at the very least a distraction from reality through romantic thinking.
10. Next, they twist it to make their depression or anger your fault

or your responsibility.

11. There is an attempt to control every aspect of your life:
12. **Instigation stage**: This stage is important because it pushes you over the edge. They blame you for the relationship failure. This allows them to continue being the victim and shun any possible responsibility.

Retreat and stay: Loss of Identity

1. You will completely **lose your identity.**
2. Walk on eggshells.
3. Think it is all your fault.
4. Blame yourself and beat yourself up.
5. Try harder.
6. You become emotionally unstable as they convince you every day… "You are crazy!"
7. You doubt your intuition because they tell you your perceptions are wrong.
8. If you start to figure things out, they switch game plans.
9. You feel like their pet they dropped off at the shelter or on the side of the road.

10. Your goal is to return to the passion phase of "true love", but that was their pseudo-reality to get you on the hook and not within anyone's ability to recover.

***At this point, the relationship has not met their fantasy and needs to be destroyed.**

***The chase is over and lost its glitter and there needs to be a new conquest.**

***The relationship failure must be securely fixed on you, so they can justify a clear conscience and of course, play the victim for their next prey.**

This is RELATIONSHIP ADDICTION TO THE CORE!

...while evil men and imposters will go from bad to worse, deceiving and being deceived. 2 Timothy 3:13

Once they are done

Or you set up even the smallest boundary:

1. They play helpless in distress and emotionally devastated.
2. They may look for their next victim.
3. They push through every boundary.
4. If you are **not controllable**, they are upset.
5. Their warped view of love is "control".

6. But if you **are controllable**, they lose respect for you.
7. You are rejected again. It is a no-win situation….

More symptoms of a devouring relationship:

1. Passive/Aggressive behaviors
2. Anger and dominance
3. Cyclical patterns of dysfunctional thinking and behaviors
4. ***Bone throwing*** is where they pretend to return to the passion phase. This is using you as their pacifier or comforter. They may return multiple times to play the victim in between multiple other tragic relationship break-ups. They often keep empathetic past lovers on the hook, while they are bored or look for a new lover to chase. If emotional tragedy strikes them and you have wiped their slate clean and forgiven them… they will return to repeat the cycle again. You have trained them to come back to you to *self-regulate*. Just depends upon how many meatless bones you are willing to chew.

Understand: They are completely incapable of loving you!

Exercise

Evaluate your main relationships.

IDENTIFYING DEVOURING BEHAVIORS

Devouring Behaviors	
1. Vanity.	
2. Searching for compliments.	
3. Heart of a hunter/pursuer.	
4. Never satisfied or content.	
5. Unable to ever love you because they love themselves too much and yet are very insecure.	
6. Frequent pity parties galore; moody.	
7. Emotional intensity alternating with instability.	
8. Manipulating master.	
9. Refuses to accept responsibility.	
10. String of past broken relationships.	
• Excuse making.	
• Intense/consuming/passion.	

• Control freaks.	
• Lack of respect for others.	
• Surrounded by others who tell them what they want to hear.	
• A real actor/actress.	
• Flirtatious.	
• Attention seeking.	
• RECKLESS	

Too Good to be True:
1. Hot passion… beware of lust.
2. Lust drives intense emotions.
3. Intense lust can be a sister to explosive anger.
4. Watch for road rage when they are driving.
5. Verbalization of excuse making, blaming and anger against authority figures: parents, teachers, employers, police, etc.

Emotional Identifying Markers	
1. Whining & complaining	
2. Confusion	
3. Demanding	
4. Withdrawing	
5. Unappeasable	
6. Talks negatively about old lovers.	
7. Obsessive thinking	
8. Daydreaming	
9. Fantasy-vacation exploits	
10. Replays past offenses.	
11. Guilt and shame drive them from reality.	
12. They make up their own reality.	
13. Lack responsibility to identify and work on their own issues.	
14. Everything is someone else's fault.	
15. Seek lots of sympathy. Builds offenses quickly.	

Application

Why can't they love you?

1. They are enamored with themselves and possibly adorned in fine clothes (to hide their insecurities).

People will be lovers of themselves, lovers of money, boastful, proud, abusive, disobedient to their parents, ungrateful, unholy, without love, unforgiving, slanderous, without self-control, brutal, not lovers of the good, treacherous, rash, conceited, lovers of pleasure rather than lovers of God—having a form of godliness but denying its power. **Have nothing to do with them.** *2 Timothy 3:2-5*

2. They look at themselves often in a mirror.

3. Emotionally immature. They get their feelings hurt easily and pout or are moody.

4. They are incomplete as a person.

5. They have a **divided, idolatrous heart and soul.** *Their heart is deceitful (divided), and now they must bear their guilt. The Lord will demolish their altars and destroy their sacred stones (images). Hosea 10:2*

6. They walk in darkness which means they have no real vision for their future. *Your eye is the lamp of your body. When your eyes are good, your whole body also is full of*

light. But when they are bad, your body also is full of darkness. See to it, then, that the light within you is not darkness. Luke 11:34-35

7. They are double-minded and unstable. *He is* <u>*double-minded*</u> *man,* <u>*unstable*</u> *in all he does. James 1:8*

Potentially you can still be valuable to them. They will think of a new plot and set up strategies to suck you in emotionally. The lure used is recapturing the intensity of the relationship you enjoyed at the beginning. When you take the bait and they get what they want, you are once again used and discarded.

Then the elaborate plan begins it is all your fault. After all, accepting responsibilities or respecting your boundaries is not even visible skill on their radar.

This is called a *man-eater or a womanizer* but basically you are devouring another for your ego supply. *Indulgence is intense sexual activity for self-gratification called hyper-sexualized.*

Possibly, neither of you have enough maturity to be in a healthy relationship and are both emotionally unavailable. Possibly you have never known healthy connection and can only feel connected with sexual activity. Back-up and develop your identity in Christ, find maturity and stability within yourself.

Healthy relationships are sacrifice, servanthood and other-centered.

Principle

Relationship addictions suck the life out of you.

Conclusion

Walk in your recovery one day at a time. Understand your addiction to relationships is destructive. **Emotional immaturity is the center of the problem that empowers the addiction cycle.** Speak truth in love. Make others earn your trust. This needs to be at least a two-year healing journey. Do not tolerate any anger, or manipulation towards you or from you towards another or yourself.

Lord, my relationships are painful. I attract toxicity. Help me to stay focused on you and my healing so I can be a whole person. Help me to identify where I devour or harm others. Help me to repent quickly and to be slow with new relationships. Give me the self-control that I need to do this and help me to set up strong accountability partners that love me and help me learn to trust my instincts. Help me to have a healthy support system that can help me build a strong foundation so I can safely grow and mature. Amen.

LESSON 8

RECOVERY FROM RELATIONSHIP ADDICTION

Addictive relationships never bring health or healing.

Introduction

You can only control yourself. Attempting to control others will drive you crazy. If the relationship is violent or destructive, it is time to receive good counsel and step back physically and emotionally. Then, you can determine what is best for you.

Addictive relationships will not usually start to recover without a crisis.

The crisis can be good. It can force you to look at reality and make a plan that looks different for your future. **If you stay in an addictive relationship pattern, you will not like who you become.**

There may be a period that you cannot emotionally handle saying no and seeing another suffer from their own insecurities. Most of our enabling behaviors are because we struggle to let another person suffer. But a period to allow them to grow and mature and make good choices without you is healthy. Protect your recovery.

Make your choices based upon what is best for you in the long term. However, they have treated you in the past is likely how they will treat you in the future without radical personal awareness of their behaviors and voluntarily seeking to grow and change. All promises without action are called *future faking* to bait you back on the hook.

Lesson

Escape the Relationship Addiction Cycle
1. Heal your inner self.
2. Know what you want in a partner.
3. Know what you will and will not tolerate.
4. Understanding relationship addiction patterns.

5. Have strong healthy boundaries.
6. Say no often. Build your own identity.
7. Push back on any dominance.
8. Correct any immature victim mentality on both sides.
9. Accept responsibility for your actions.
10. Don't make yourself too available.
11. Don't answer texts quickly and see if the person has a meltdown and if they are disrespectful of your time.
12. Voice your opinions and see if they are respected or reshaped.
13. Be slow to make decisions.

Maturing
1. Work on your own emotional maturity.
2. Recognize intense lust creates dysfunctional relationships.
3. Recognize your passive/aggressive behaviors called *push-pull.*
4. Surround yourself with accountability.
5. Face your past, so, your future can look different.
6. Stop denying.
7. Find safe people.

8. Ask accountability partners to expose your blind spots.
9. Find a servant's heart (not with the person you are addicted to, but with those near your circle of influence: elderly parents, children, co-workers, friends, handicapped or elderly neighbors).

Next step:

Work a Recovery Program
1. Find safe relationships worth investing in.
2. Realize if you have developed devouring behaviors.
3. Understand how your relationship failures repeat themselves.
4. Recognize any over-reacting emotionally to situations as a signal to deal with your unhealed wounds.
5. Work on becoming a whole person.
6. Develop your own identity.
7. Attend a love and sex addiction recovery meeting and just listen.
8. Real relationships are <u>not fairytales</u>, they are work with lots of struggles.

Dear friends, I urge you, as aliens and strangers in the world, to abstain from sinful desires (fleshly lusts), which war against your soul. 1 Peter 2:11

Is there any hope for a marriage like this?

It is helpful to recognize these behaviors, so you can detach from your emotions and stop the manipulation and dominance. **Healthy boundaries are often met with the other person ending the relationship. But at least you know, it was not real love.** You must empower yourself to be able to set boundaries. A boundary isn't a real boundary if another person can violate it and you have no power to implement a consequence and have no resolve to enforce it. Work on financially empowering yourself so you are free to choose to stay or go.

If a person truly changes, they will be responsible, submit to counseling, accountability partners, and consistently works a recovery program to heal their past wounds, it is possible for them to recover. But this is a lot of work. Underneath these behaviors is a very wounded soul. They must recognize their dysfunction and determine to heal and change. Only they can make those decisions.

The best thing you can do is to work on your own recovery and accountability program. This will either propel the other person into a recovery program or will cause the situation to **escalate. Addictive relationships never bring health or healing. This is just**

another form of addiction.

Exercise

Is it a Game?	
1. Are they truly repentant or just sorry for the consequences?	
2. Do they have a short and long-term plan for recovery?	
3. Are they dealing with the real problems or just the consequences?	
4. Do they have an accountability partner or a recovery group?	
5. Are they willingly under authority with a good attitude: courts, family, employment, school, etc.?	
6. Have they accepted full responsibility for their poor choices without complaining?	
7. Who received the last financial consequence for their poor decision you or your loved one?	
8. Are they hiding anything?	
9. Are they developing accountability groups and a support team?	
10. Are they choosing healthy friends?	
11. Are they making restitution for past offenses?	
12. Do they respect your boundaries? Are you able to safely say no and be accepted?	

13. Are they serving others and giving back to their family and community?	
14. Do they consistently repeat a cycle of regret alternating with behavioral relapse of abuse? If so, they need stronger boundaries and/or harder consequences.	

Work on sober expectations of relationships, not fairytales.

Positive Behaviors Indicative of Recovery
1. Building relationships where there is mutual sharing and support.
2. Grieving after relapse and voluntarily setting up stronger accountability.
3. Willingly submits to one another in love, respect, and kindness.

Possible Needs
1. You may want to use a third party to rebuild the relationship.
2. Anger management skills may be necessary.
3. Money management skills may be necessary.
4. Someone monitoring the situation who is not emotionally invested in the outcome.

5. Someone who is authoritarian enough to hold me accountable with tough consequences when I set up my boundaries and then violate them myself.

> *When it comes to relationship recovery, do not expect perfection but do require progress.*

Application

Accountability
Sometimes addictive family relationships need more boundaries.
1. Keeping our financial accounts open to the scrutiny of another who understands addiction. Make a budget. Learn money management skills.
2. Keeping all your phone calls with toxic relationships on speaker phone for others to hold you accountable to not be sucked in again.
3. Keep all your visits short or with a trusted friend or companion with you if you share parenting and must go interact with them.
4. No physical or verbal contact for a specified period may be needed.
5. Letter writing for 30 days to a year may be appropriate if this person is incarcerated or you share parenting responsibilities, or they are a verbally abusive family member.

Identify what you want in a relationship and refuse nonsense.

Qualities for Healthy Relationship
1. Loyal and faithful
2. Dependable
3. Good to parents, sibling, friends, and animals
4. Compassionate
5. Kind with good manners
6. Teachable
7. Goal oriented
8. Respectful
9. Good provider, protective,
10. Servant leadership
11. Good reputation
List other qualities you are looking for in a partner:

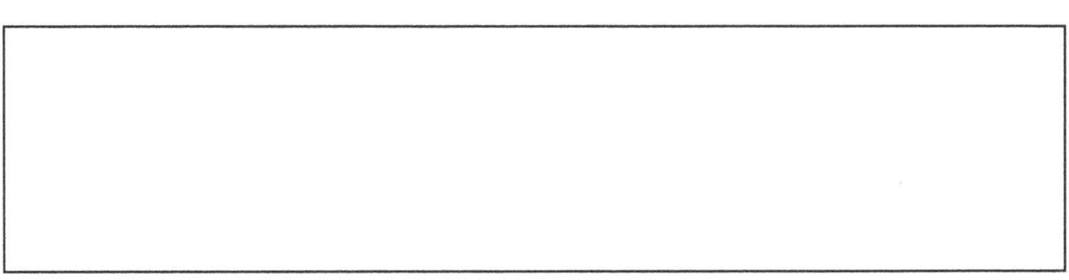

> *Have courage and trust the recovery process.*

Principle

Addictive relationships never bring health or healing.

Conclusion

Work a plan to not enable others to stay on a destructive path. Enabling and excuse making can cause a quick slide into an *addictive relationship relapse.* In early addiction recovery, a relationship addiction may trigger one or both people to go back into life threatening substance use disorder.

This is the plight of most domestic violent relationships. It is difficult to escape if a relationship has become an addiction. You give away your power to gain power over another. You don't have an identity and develop an identity in someone else and then think if they leave you have lost yourself.

Instead, study and heal insecure attachment behaviors. It takes great courage to take a step back from our controlling and manipulating outcomes.

In recovery, we need someone to monitor all our decisions regarding our toxic relationships. In early substance use disorder recovery, we cannot trust our own judgment. **Our people-picker is broken.** Abstain from relationships for at least a year. If you are prone to relationship addiction patterns and have previously relapsed after a break-up, a two-year waiting period would be much better. You would have time to work on your own recovery and then sustain it or actively teach it to others.

Father, be my advocate. I can't even see the forest for the trees. I don't know which way to go. I wake up with anxiety and my empathy is too strong for others who abuse me. I forget and repeat my failures. Forgive me. Help me to heal. Without you, this is impossible. Be my father, be my God. Deliver me from all my addictive patterns. Amen.

LESSON 9

DISTANCE EVALUATOR

Painful relationships need distance to bring peace and perspective.

Introduction

When we are entangled in a relationship with active addiction or enabling behaviors, think about space and distance. Move back to a safe and comfortable level. If the relationship is still causing stress and anxiety, move back further. Your inner circle should be reserved for people who have earned the right to be there.

The purpose of distance is to bring peace and allow perspective. This lets you focus on others who want and need your help. You must also discern if this person will accept correction or if this is an abusive person entrenched in demanding their own way.

Lesson

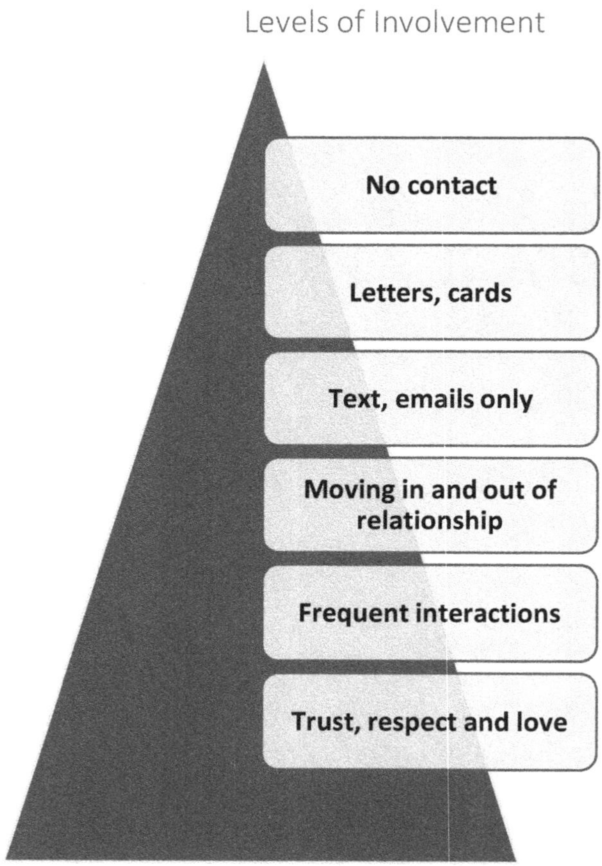

Levels of Involvement

No contact

Letters, cards

Text, emails only

Moving in and out of relationship

Frequent interactions

Trust, respect and love

No contact

- When a person with abusive behaviors is blaming everyone else for their problems and refusing personal responsibility, they need the space to sit with the consequences of their own decisions. This will look different in different situations. It also may be temporary. It could last for a few hours, days or even need to last a year or more. Always receive counseling or group support at this level.
- Always establish accountability and relationship rules before re-entering this relationship.
- If they are lying, stealing, manipulating, bullying or will not listen to reason, you need space to heal.
- A key to the necessity of this measure being exercised is when the relationship has turned to *total torment*. You can't think of anything else, and it wakes you up at night with fear, anxiety, or misery. For your own safety and sanity, create distance and space for yourself to heal.
- If this has been a toxic unhealthy lover or a relationship with previous domestic violence and now you are obsessing over them, this is called *limerence*. Limerence is a clear sign of a relationship built on a *trauma bond*. No contact is the best option for you to heal. All contact, if necessary, should include a third party.

Letters and cards

- This is a space where the relationship is valuable, and you would like to keep the door open for future healing.
- Or reconciliation isn't likely, but you would like to show continued love and support without enabling or being wounded physically or emotionally.

Text and emails only

- Some loved ones caught in addiction and enablers are so relationally dependent that there is constant, compulsive enabling in the relationship, for your sake, distance is needed but you may not be able to completely let go. If you must communicate, include a non-emotional third-party in all your communication. The third-party needs to have your best interest at heart to *prevent you from being sucked in, which is called hoovering*. As soon as you are sucked back in, the mistreatment starts again. If you are relationally addicted to the person and have a strong empath muscle, you will not be able to communicate with this person without the cycle of abuse starting again. The cycle begins with *love bombing* to pull you back in with *unrealistic promises this is called future faking.*

Moving in and out of relationship

- This space is for a person who is learning to manage their own emotions.

- Anyone who reacts, responds, or makes decisions based upon emotions need a strong, dependable loved one to say, "You may not engage me until you have worked through some of these intense emotions, then we can talk."
- Sometimes exaggerated emotions are justified, and they need to talk through the confusion of the day, but if the emotions are being used to violate the trust in the relationship or build a case to manipulate others emotionally, blame, or make excuses, there needs to be distance.
- Detaching emotionally and letting go of outcomes is a process in our healing journey.

Frequent Interactions

- This is a space for loved ones who are finding their recovery path in life. They need encouragement and emotional support and direction, but also need the space to build self-confidence. This will be reserved for those who are accepting responsibility for their past actions and making restitution and doing the work to grow with support groups and accountability. *Their words and actions will match.*
- In this space, we will see our loved ones reach out to counselors, sponsors, and valuable mentors to develop other healthy relationships.

Trust, Respect, and Love

- Do not allow anyone into your inner circle who cannot be fully trusted.
- Do not allow anyone in your inner circle who does not respect your opinion, decisions, and boundaries.
- Do not give your love away to someone who will trample it and abuse you.

> *DISTANCE YOURSELF EMOTIONALLY from unteachable ones who refuse to change.*

Exercise

1. Distance yourself from those whose lives are disorderly. *...that you withdraw yourselves from every person that walks disorderly...1 Thessalonians 4:6*
2. Do not worry about another adult's self-imposed problems. It will only bring you suffering. **Mind your own business**. *You should mind your own business and work with your hands...so you won't be dependent on anybody. 1 Thessalonians 4:11b-12b*
3. Work on being "quiet" inside your heart and find work you enjoy. *And to make your ambition to lead a quiet life: 1 Thessalonians 4:11a*
4. Take notice of the person who is willful, wayward, and unruly and distance yourself from them that they may desire to

correct themselves. *Warn a divisive person once, and then warn them a second time. After that, have nothing to do with them. Titus 3:10*

5. Do not count this person as an enemy, but as a loved one who needs to be corrected and held accountable. *If any man obeys not our word by this epistle, note that man, and have no company with him, that he may be ashamed. Yet count him not as an enemy but admonish him as a brother. 2 Thessalonians 3:14-15*
6. Do not allow your thoughts to be consumed with the consequences of other's choices. Think about the situation for 5 minutes. If it isn't your problem and there is no power in your hands to stop or change the behaviors that keep causing the problems, push it out of your mind and enjoy your day!

Tip: I literally set a timer for 5 minutes. After 5 minutes, I stop thinking about the problem, detach, and let it go. Letting other adults handle their own problems and/or consequences to their poor choices is emotional maturity for you and them.

Application

DISTANCE EVALUATOR

Do we need relationship distance? Ask Yourself:

1. Does this person attempt to control my thoughts?	
2. Does this person dominate or regulate my actions?	
3. Is there a repeated pattern of abuse?	
4. Does this person attempt to make themselves financially dependent on me or make me dependent upon them?	
5. Does this person have constant excuses for why they can't work or keep a job?	
6. Are they irresponsible? (Poor work ethic, poor student, delinquent on child support, etc.)	
7. Do they overspend on eating out, cigarettes, vapes, and entertainment?	
8. Do they have poor money management skills?	
9. Does their money disappear everyday: fee, fine, robbery, suspicious expenses?	
10. Does this person lie to me?	
11. Are others (who love me) concerned about my over involvement with this person?	
12. Do they flatter me and smile to get my	

devotion?	
13. Do they play the victim and act helpless and come to me for deliverance?	
14. **Most importantly: Am I free to say "NO" to them without repercussions.**	

Could it possibly be this person's manipulation is steeped in ***mind control****? This means you have lost your identity and are now being controlled by fear or other strong emotions.* Do you believe the false promises of a future of peace and love? Do they flip your words and say you said things you didn't say? Do they assume your motives are selfish?

> *When you are free from a toxic relationship, stand steadfast and do not be entangled again with them. Toxic relationships makes you captive in the bondage of confusion. Galatians 5:1*

BONES

Does your loved one throw you a bone? Watch for these subtle techniques of manipulation which keep you coming back. The bone is a <u>pretense action</u> or statement to give you the love, respect, and comfort you deserve.

Watch out! Once you take the bait, you will be entangled again in their game and the manipulative rebel reappears. It is important to see their actions and discern their motives and not to listen to cheap words.

Trauma Bonds form in a sick cycle of push-pull from an abandonment/neglect cycle usually from childhood trauma. Start making mental notes of the unhealthy cycles in the relationship.

Subtle Tricks of the Chameleon

This person is an opportunist, they use a different bone by being a different chameleon with every new opportunity. Chameleon can change colors to match his environment.

When he is with:

- A police officer, they identify with them by becoming an informant.
- Grandparent, they act like helpless sixteen-year-old victim.
- With their Christian aunt, they quote Scriptures and pretend to be converted.
- Drug dealers, they pretend to be a bully and a thug.
- A lover will vacillate between intense loving passion and physical and verbal dominance.
- *Verbal dominance is where a person repeats themselves continually louder and longer to force their sick reality onto another.*
- *Bully/victim game. A bully will bully you with dominance*

tactics. And then play a victim with others to get sympathy. Just about the time you are sick of their bullying.... they become the victim.

- *Victim/bully game. Now they play the victim with you to hook in your sympathy and suck you into agreeing with them and meeting their needs. Then they go bully another immediately after this. Next, they play the victim with you again. Watch for these cycles.*

Principle

Painful relationships need distance to bring peace and perspective.

Conclusion

My motto here is **"Don't feed the bears."** When a bear approaches a car and acts sweet to get food, he will become aggressive when your food runs out and you have to say "no". A person with severe relational addiction behaviors can be the same way. They may appear sweet, innocent, and hungry. But if you consistently give emotionally, physically, sexually, financially, to one that is relationally toxic, they will expect it. Expect to be bullied when you have to say "no" to their demands to preserve yourself.

In conclusion, the root of the problem is a lack of personal identity and accountability. The emotional immature individual has not developed a strong sense of self and personal boundaries usually because of childhood trauma or neglect.

Therefore, whoever is the object of obsession becomes our new identity and we will become intensely involved in each other's life in a pleasant way at first and then in a dominant and controlling way. Because we lack identity and secure attachments, we tend to consume and control others.

Lord, help me to build a strong and safe identity in you. Let me find healthy vibrant relationships that I can enjoy. Help me to set strong boundaries and move in and out of toxic relationships at a level that is safe. Guard me and keep me in your love. Amen.

LESSON 10

OVERCOMING LUST PATTERNS

Self-absorption misses true love and drops into lust.

Introduction

Lust patterns dominate unintentional thinking patterns just like any other addiction. Lust can force itself upon you or be a hard pattern to break. There is no way to stop it without intentionally recognizing the thought pattern, refusing, and replacing it with a healthy thought. Practice conquering lustful thoughts to build the skills to conquer other addictive thinking patterns. Practice self-control in other areas of your life to develop the ability to say no to yourself.

Those who are newly sober can be doing very well unless they are triggered by an addictive sexual relationship, then their recovery may crash. There is a pleasure center in the brain triggered by lust, sex, porn, food, drugs, alcohol, or any other addiction. It all triggers' addictive brain patterns. Early recovery relationships also trigger intense abandonment wounds.

If we can learn the skills to change one thinking pattern, we can change another. Otherwise, one dominating uncontrolled pattern may lead to the next.

Lesson

Skills to Conquer Lust
1) Refusing feelings as a guide, not denying them, but not following them.
2) When lust comes, make a prayer target for the person that is the object of your lust. Lord, give them purity and safety. Help me see them through eyes of virtue and protection and not devouring.
3) Practice refusing the thought …by taking dominion over the ground in your head.
4) Set an intention to practice self-control. Don't even look.
5) Play it out to emotional destruction, not the pleasure.
6) Think of others who will be hurt.
7) How would this interfere with your life goals?
8) Practice self-discipline in other areas of life.
9) Purpose to do what is right

10) Break its power through confession with one or two trusted friends.
11) Think about habits, patterns, past coping skills… has this been a dysfunctional thinking pattern before.
12) Set an intention for each day (peace, contentment, joy).
13) Have a motto to refocus yourself when your thoughts stray.
14) Learn to meditate upon your breath. The only thing you can really control. Then observe your thoughts, but don't identify with them or indulge them. Only observe.

Lust is likely not only triggering a pleasure center of your brain but giving your imagination a place to focus with a sense of control. Could the root cause of lust be an attempt to control one area of life because other areas are imbalanced and out of control?

In a fantasy, you can control what the other person says or does and the scenario to validate, affirm or nurture yourself in ways that are lacking.

Our imaginations are a good thing when they are sanctified and directed towards creativity. Control is a good thing when it helps us develop self-control. *Unsanctified use of imagination* or control can be like treading water and end in exhaustion or emotional drowning.

When lustful imagination controls every aspect of a fantasy relationship, it is a powerful drive to role play the acts you have envisioned to bring fulfillment of the fantasy. If the actions do not fulfill fantasy, it may drive you to despair and your next relapse. If the person can't be controlled, they may be discarded quickly.

Triggers
1) Needs of affirmation, adoration, or affection not fulfilled
2) Unmet needs, neglect, natural sex drive, unhealed wounds
3) Desperation to be loved, held, and cared for….
4) Undisciplined thinking.
Another trigger could be uncontrollable circumstances which are overwhelming emotionally and trigger old emotional wounds. .

Would this give the enemy an opportunity to slander, accuse or blaspheme the name of the Lord?

Scriptures

1) **Make no provision for the flesh.** *But put on the Lord Jesus Christ, and make no provision for the flesh, to gratify it desires. Romans 13:14*
2) **Flee youthful lust.** *Flee the evil desires of youth and pursue righteousness, faith, love, and peace, along with those who call on the Lord out of a pure heart. 2 Timothy 2:22*
3) **Can a man take fire in his lap and not be burned?** *For the price of a prostitute reduces one to a loaf of bread, and an adulteress hunts for a precious life. Can anyone take fire in his lap and his clothes not be burned? Proverbs 6:26-27*

4) **Victim mentality**… driven like a dog to return to their vomit through animal like instincts. *As a dog returns to its vomit, fools repeat their folly. Proverbs 26:11*

Devastation Trap
Justifying,
Rationalizing….
Everyone else does it.
No one will know.
It can be a secret.
We are adults.

Ungodly Soul tie vs.	Godly Spiritual tie
-Sensual -Selfish -Idolatrous -Sexual -Potential to shipwreck your whole life and leave you stranded.	-Security -Stability -Sacrifice -Safe -Sacrifice your desires to God

If lust is in your dreams or your early sleep/wake state then it is in your subconscious and needs pulled up and renounced, rejected, and not indulged. It must be dealt with immediately. Find what triggered it. **Emotional rejection can cause a self-comforting role-**

playing imaginary romance. If it is a dominate subconscious habitual thought pattern, it will demand to be played out.

Does confession increase its power because you are looking to have it excused, approved, and/or validated?

Does replaying it lead to rationalizing, reasoning, and manipulating to convince yourself its ok?

What makes it stronger, what makes it weaker?

Rules to Live By
1. Do not give anyone false expectations of a future if you don't intend on pursuing the happily ever after.
2. Do not have multiple relationships going at the same time.
3. Do not sleep with the roommate.

4.	Do not rally others to fight over you.
5.	Do not chase them until you catch them and then dump them.
6.	Do not lure someone away from their stable relationships for a short fling.
7.	Do not withhold emotional connection with an intimate marriage partner.

Sacrificial love
1) Heals lust
2) Fills the soul
3) Leads to contentment
4) Worth the wait
5) Doesn't have to worry about hurting others
6) Doesn't have to worry about exposure.

Identifying True Love!
1 Corinthians 13
• Love never fails.
• This love grows and grows with time.
• Never remembers wrongs.
• Thinks the best.
• Deep Spiritual Connection
• Never remembers wrongs.

Thinks the best.
One accord.
One mind.
One heart.
Love covers a multitude of sins.
True love will care for each other without fail as a privilege and will be happy to do it.

1 Corinthians 13:4-8 NIV

Love is patient, love is kind. It does not envy, it does not boast, it is not proud. [5] It does not dishonor others, it is not self-seeking, it is not easily angered, it keeps no record of wrongs. [6] Love does not delight in evil but rejoices with the truth. [7] It always protects, always trusts, always hopes, always perseveres. [8] Love never fails. But where there are prophecies, they will cease; where there are tongues, they will be stilled; where there is knowledge, it will pass away.

Romans 5:5 NIV

And hope does not put us to shame, because God's love has been poured out into our hearts through the Holy Spirit, who has been given to us.

2 Corinthians 13:11 NIV

Finally, brothers and sisters rejoice! Strive for full restoration, encourage one another, be of one mind, live in peace. And the God of love and peace will be with you.

Exercise

Gut honesty leads to more intimacy. It is so important to be seen, heard, accepted, and loved. Confess your lust or infidelity to a safe trusted person with a desire to repent and escape it.

Warning: Sometimes, it is more important not to confess your significant other (if they are immature or clingy and lack confidence). Clearing your conscience is less important than protecting others who will be hurt by your actions or misjudge your motives.

True Love Evaluation	
1) Can this person withstand the test of time?	
2) Relationships will not develop a firm foundation on lust or neediness.	
3) True love is always loving-kindness.	
4) Laying down your life in love… sacrificially dying to selfishness.	
5) Feel their burdens… like a type of love we have for our kids.	

6) Its meditative, relaxing, and deep breathing, rarely stressful.	
7) Safe	
8) Can't be forced	
9) Can't be rushed or grabbed too quickly	
10) Baby chick or a butterfly… it must struggle to be birthed to be strong.	
11) Thinks of the other one first.	
12) Go through the fire in the relationship.	
13) Goes in the fire through the love of Christ.	

Trust Bond
1) Simple love develops with simple child-like trust
2) No inhibitions
3) No fear to love
4) No fear to let go
5) No fear to spend or be spent for one another
6) Sacrifices are mutual, not one-sided
7) There is an equal give and take
8) Best Friends
9) No need to hide
10) Always willing to wait.
11) Individuality is respected.

12) Boundaries are accepted.

Fear Bond
1) Stubborn
2) Refuses to connect except temporarily to get their needs met.
3) Build hard exterior walls around their heart.
4) Refuses to connect through intimate conversation.
5) Refuses correction
6) Avoids deep intimacy
7) Feels unsafe
8) Expects to be betrayed
9) Embraces depression
10) Isolates
11) Distracts themselves with television, games, social media.
12) Attaches to inanimate objects.
13) Possessions much more important than people
14) Angry/bullish if confronted
15) Expects rejection
16) Lonely

Application

Seek God first and you will find the connection you need and desire. *Let the Lord freely move people in and out of your life.* If you are not needy, you will be less impulsive and less likely to stumble into a repetitive cycle of broken relationships. Take the time to nurture yourself and then nurture a friendship before you allow romance to develop.

When I develop a love relationship with my heavenly Father, I am strong enough to love another. Love God first and then others through your identity of wholeness with the Father. When I am broken and starving for love, I am needy, and rush and confusion is very near, and I forget to include the Lord.

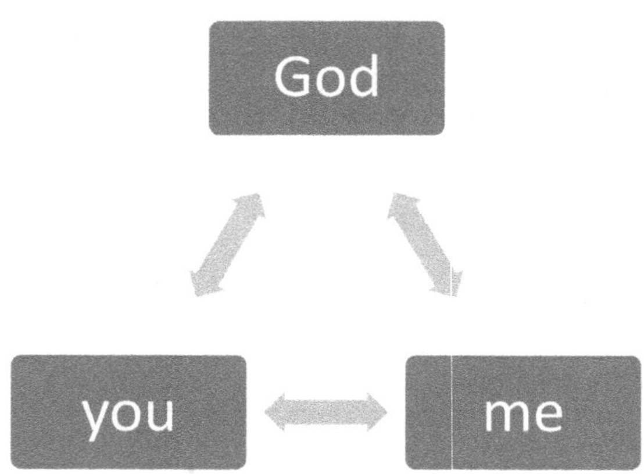

Principle

Self-absorption misses true love and drops into lust.

Conclusion

Give God permission to act supernaturally in your life and intervene. Then do the work to build your life in Christ to develop the skills to enjoy healthy relationships.

Building Internal Controls
1) Confession to a sponsor or trusted friend
2) Self-denial
3) Sacrifice needs to God
4) Prayer and fasting
5) Abiding in Christ
=More than a conqueror! *Romans 8:37 NIV* *No, in all these things we are more than conquerors through him who loved us.*

Lord, will you give me the desire to conquer my lust. Lust has been a close friend that has replaced true intimacy in my life. I have not learned to trust others and attract others as broken as myself. Help me to see my worth through your eyes and not my own. Help me to know your love for me. Enlarge my heart that I may trust enough to receive blessings from you and others. Amen

LESSON 11

THE CHASE OF THE FANTASY

A wounded inner core develops fantasy thinking to escape reality and ends in disgrace.

Introduction

Indulging the obsession

Everything you think you need is in this person. They are a fantasy god, a deliverer. They distract you from the emotional pain inside, from the rejection of past lovers. For a moment, they fill the void of abandonment and neglect through your imagination.

Night after night you feel their presence in your imagination. In your mind, you are obsessed and just need to conquer this obsession and play it out so it will manifest or resolve.

But this kind of passion is tricky. It tricks you to the very core and makes you do things that would be unthinkable.

You can do it all to fulfill a fantasy, it won't matter. *The other person cannot be held any better than you can hold the wind.* It isn't real. It's just a *fantasy obsession.*

Have you done this before? No matter how much you serve, how much you love, care, dote, prepare, desire, dream… they aren't emotionally there. It's your imagination silly. They are just human. And maybe even a foolish avoidant or controlling person without any skills to love you back. Recognize this pattern of obsession as *toxic replay.*

Lesson

Wounded ones divided and are willing to accept a partial plate.
1. Forgive yourself.
2. Recommit to protect yourself.
3. Rededicate yourself to your future goals.
4. Save yourself for a strong partner who is available to love you.
5. Force yourself to go slow with new relationships.

Dating Match

1. Intelligence	
2. Socially	
3. Financially	
4. Physical-Health	
5. Spiritual Zeal	
6. Mutual Interest	
7. Energy level	

Do not divide and devalue yourself and accept a partial plate. If you have done this, own your part in it and forgive yourself. Recommit to your value and look inside to heal your emotional self. If you develop a relationship with imbalance, it may still be satisfying but will need much more work and two willing teachable partners.

Sexual Obsessing

1. Sexual fantasy as a teen or young adult without maturity and skills to stop obsessing will eventually end acting out the fantasy.

Sexual encounters can fall short of fantasy and lead to deeper sexual perversions to satisfy. This always leads to future *relationship discontent. Never satisfied are the eyes of man. Proverbs 27:20*

2. Deep sexual obsession develops an imaginary lover. This lover is your friend, and you speak to them or imagine them as perfect. Everything that happens in the fantasy: what is said, what is

done, how they feel about you, how they validate you, their mood is all within your control.

Now when I develop an attempt to develop this relationship with the person that is the object of my obsession, **there is major control issues.**

3. Sexual players move quick. The player expects intimacy, trust, perfection right away. Soon they become addicted to the person and quickly the relationship takes over their life, thoughts, and time. This person loses their own identity quickly. The relationship can't sustain this level of excitement and heat.

The couple become emotionally entangled quickly and this leads to confusion. Insecure attachment style of vacillation *push-pull* behaviors is common. Come here, no, go away. I want you, no, I don't want you.

Without your own identity and the emotional health to allow the other person their own identity, you will engage another only to consume them. When that person doesn't fulfill your fantasy, the relationship is over, and you are deeply disappointed. Without insight, healing, and intentionality, you will just do it again.

Stop Obsessing
Tell me how to control obsessing and how to stop it.
1. Take every thought captive. Tear down strongholds.
2. Meditate upon my word day and night.

3. Practice self-control.
4. Stop the thought in 3 seconds. Renounce it.
5. Cry to God for help. Read the Word. Pray for help.
6. Slow down, journal.
The confusion of it will stop when you are ready to refuse it and take dominion over your thought life…

Outcome of Relationship Addiction
• Feelings of defeat with a negative internal critic
• Self-destructive thinking=relapse or suicide
• Depression, confusion, loss
• Devastation and death of a long-term fantasy
• Disappointment, despair, and disgrace
• Potential violence-If I can't have you, no one can.

Exercise

Development of Emotional Skills
1) Look for reasons (losses, lack of nurturing, validation, painful circumstances, domestic violence) for sexual fantasy.
2) Heal your inner wounds.
3) Find other ways to meet unfulfilled needs.
4) Move the fantasy into healthier creative passions.

Application

Fantasy vs Reality

Fantasy surely isn't reality. Because when I play the fantasy it ends in love, it doesn't end up in rejection and feeling abandoned and like I have certainly lost my mind.

Fairytale Promises
1) You are going to be known, seen, heard, held, validated, valued, with affirmation and affection.
2) You will have a life partner that will understand you.
3) You will be the apple of their eye and the center of their attention and vice versa.
4) The two of you will be like the doves with a lifetime of cooing and preening.
5) The heart-to-heart connection will be real.
6) The passion will be real and unending. The thing you always look forward to.
7) They will always want to hold and kiss you.
8) True love will grow, and the connection will be magnetic and unstoppable and will never end.
9) Things will magically work out.

There is no obsessing over another person that will end in fulfilling lasting love. This feels so familiar, but it is a toxic attraction to brokenness. Starting relationships with obsessing (limerence) is likely to end poorly. You are more likely to end up hating the person.

Consider this story, Amnon, King David's son. He was the half-brother of Tamar and desired her. He plotted to get her alone. Then he forced himself on her and raped her. As soon as he had done this thing, his obsessive love for her turned to hate and he despised her. His complete rejection of her after he stole her innocence was more damaging to her than the forceable rape.

Physical violation can be easier to recover from than an emotional violation.

---

2 Samuel 13:1-19 NIV

In the course of time, Amnon, son of David, fell in love with Tamar, the beautiful sister of Absalom, son of David. [2] Amnon became so obsessed with his sister Tamar that he made himself ill. She was a virgin, and it seemed impossible for him to do anything to her. [3] Now Amnon had an adviser named Jonadab son of Shimeah, David's brother. Jonadab was a very shrewd man. [4] He asked Amnon, "Why do you, the king's son, look so haggard morning after morning? Won't you tell me?" Amnon said to him, "I'm in love with Tamar, my brother Absalom's sister." [5] "Go to bed and pretend to be ill," Jonadab said. "When your father comes to see you, say to him, 'I would like my sister Tamar to come and give me something to eat. Let her prepare the food in my sight so I may watch her and then eat it from her hand.'" [6] So Amnon lay down and pretended to be ill. When the king came to see him, Amnon said to him, "I would like my sister Tamar to come and make some special bread in my sight, so I may eat from her hand." [7] David sent word to Tamar at the palace: "Go to the house of your brother Amnon and prepare some food for him." [8] So Tamar went to the house of her brother Amnon, who was lying down. She took some dough, kneaded it, made the bread in his sight, and baked it. [9] Then she took the pan and served him the bread, but he refused to eat. "Send everyone out of here," Amnon said. So, everyone left him. [10] Then Amnon said to Tamar, "Bring the food here into my bedroom so I may eat from your hand." And Tamar took the bread she had prepared and brought it to her brother Amnon in his bedroom. [11] But when she took it to him to eat, he grabbed her and said, "Come to bed with me, my sister." [12] "No, my brother!" she said to him. "Don't force me! Such a thing should not be done in Israel! Don't do this wicked thing. [13] What about me? Where could I get rid of my disgrace? And what about you? You would be like one of the wicked fools in Israel. Please speak to the king; he will not keep me from being married to you." [14] But he refused to listen to her, and since he was stronger than she, he raped her. [15] Then Amnon hated her with intense hatred. In fact, he hated her more than he had loved her. Amnon said to her, "Get up and get out!" [16] "No!" she said to him. "Sending me away would be a greater wrong than what you have already done to me." But he refused to listen to her. [17] He called his personal servant and said, "Get this woman out of my sight and bolt the door after her." [18] So his servant put her out and bolted the door after her. She was wearing an ornate robe, for this was the kind of garment the virgin daughters of the king wore. [19] Tamar put ashes on her head and tore the ornate robe she was wearing. She put her hands on her head and went away, weeping aloud as she went.

Amnon's love for his half-sister was obviously not love, but a form of obsessive limerence. It tormented him to the point of deception, lying and selfish, self-centered abuse of someone who was innocent. His obsession to satisfy his fantasy was stronger than his desire to protect and honor his half-sister.

2 Samuel 13:20-22,28 NIV

And Tamar lived in her brother Absalom's house, a desolate woman. [21] When King David heard all this, he was furious. [22] And Absalom never said a word to Amnon, either good or bad; he hated Amnon because he had disgraced his sister Tamar. [28] Absalom ordered his men, "Listen! When Amnon is in high spirits from drinking wine and I say to you, 'Strike Amnon down,' then kill him. Don't be afraid. Haven't I given you this order? Be strong and brave."

Later, Tamar's brother, Absalom, avenged her and had Amnon killed. Amnon lost his life for acting upon his sexual obsession. Tamar wept loudly and was disgraced and lived her life with her brother, Absalom, a desolate woman.

Principle

A wounded inner core develops a fantasy to escape reality and ends in disgrace.

Conclusion

Possibly your sexual fantasy is so strong you cannot control yourself. You reason and rationalize it all away as acceptable. After all, maybe they are the "one", the one who will fulfill your fantasy. Nothing may be strong enough to stop you. The obsession is so powerful it feels like real love. Know this! Obsession is not love!

Think this thought. What if my actions destroy this person for their entire life. What if they feel deceived, disgraced, confused, and lost emotionally forever. Now play out this scenario and know the acting upon an obsession could end in hatred. It ends in disgrace and confusion. Surely this is enough to stop you from your selfish act.

Reality

Fantasy surely isn't reality. Because when I play the fantasy it ends in love, it doesn't end up in rejection and trigger past abandoned wounds. Fantasy has control.

Acting upon my obsession is a choice and within my control, but I am powerless over the consequences of acting it out.

Disassociation

If you have repetitive patterns in relationships that start with intense obsession, fantasy and lust and end ugly with disgrace and hatred, explore with a counselor the possibility of some disassociation from reality. Often, if you were raised in trauma with molestation or domestic violence, you will have developed a mild, moderate, or even severe disassociation pattern of thinking where you tend to live in an alternative world. This was a learned pattern of survival as a child but does not work well as an adult.

Oh Lord, I am desperate to change and feel powerless to do so. Give me the instruction to heal within my own heart that I may prepare myself for the stability of the loving, healthy relationship I desire. God, help me, or I won't survive the toxic despair of these types of relationships. Amen.

LESSON 12

RECOGNITION OF A PLAYER

True love is never dominance, control, or manipulation.

Introduction

Do you Attract Players?

Trauma bonding relationship addictions almost always attract players. Once you have met your player and had some fun, now there is a bond. It could be a fear bond or maybe an *enabling bond where you intensely focus on rescuing this person.*

Enabling bonds are steeped in rescuing others from their problems, too much empathy, too much forgiveness, excessive excuse making and controlling outcomes.

Now when reality begins to expose itself, you may have moved too fast and are now trapped, and the confusion is strong. Reality is much different than the fairytale romances this relationship may have promised at the beginning.

The player is not a derogative term. A *player* is a person with *dysfunctional relationship patterns* because of their past unhealed wounds. It is a person without a good sense of their own identity. They have difficulty self-regulating and consume or control others to regulate themselves, but this usually ends with more dysregulation.

Any of us who are emotionally sick can be the player, groomer or prey in different relationships or we may have all three types of these relationships in our lives at once. You can't heal with guilt, shame, and self-condemnation. So go easy on the judgment of yourself and others.

This information is basically to help understand patterns not to label people. Similar patterns can be in bosses, co-workers, neighbors, siblings, parents, but are usually in romantic relationships. The closer the relationship the more damage it can do. Some of us grew up with this and had no choice and never developed a sense of our own selves and then learned these behaviors for survival. Now, as an adult, we can grow, heal, and mature into healthy individuals.

Lesson

The Player: Dominance and Control	
1) You said…. Your words are flipped and used against you.	
2) You made me a promise… future talk not based upon relationship growth, or sobriety. Respect is demanded not earned.	
3) You become the object of focus… when this happens their every move is based upon what they think will make them your source in life. They may want you to be dependent upon them. You may be their new ego supply. Their attentiveness may feel magical but is steeped in control.	
4) Independence is usurped and dominance begins. There is a discussion about how you need protection, how vulnerable you are and need to be more cautious. You start to question your safety and look over your shoulder. They are the protector. The world is unsafe without them.	
5) Calls increase, text increase, they request your company daily.	
6) Aggression increases if they don't get their way. Things escalate and the other person's stability is based upon whether they can manipulate you to get what they want. <u>Often request turn into all or nothing</u>	

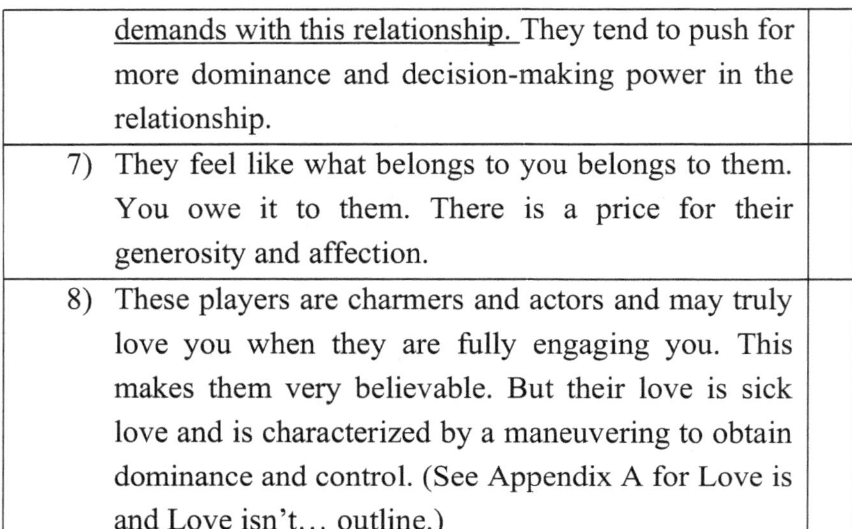

	demands with this relationship. They tend to push for more dominance and decision-making power in the relationship.	
7)	They feel like what belongs to you belongs to them. You owe it to them. There is a price for their generosity and affection.	
8)	These players are charmers and actors and may truly love you when they are fully engaging you. This makes them very believable. But their love is sick love and is characterized by a maneuvering to obtain dominance and control. (See Appendix A for Love is and Love isn't… outline.)	

Wounded people don't love themselves and are insecure and need control over others to feel secure. If you let them control you, they feel loved on the one hand, but they lose respect for you and dominate and control even more. They may be a bully one day and a victim the next. This ***bully/victim cycle*** is a manipulation game. This is after the initial fairytale love bombing phase of the relationship. You may be so confused that you lose parts of yourself attempting to regain the **original passion phase.** Next, the definition of love is skewed. It could be intense devotion, and then turn to intense jealousy. It could be a servant's heart one moment and ownership and dominance the next.

Relationship Addictions are characterized by confusion and anxiety.

Toxic love may end in domestic violence. *Domestic violence, raging, accusing, threatening, or bullying of any manner is relationship sabotage* to repeat a previous pattern in life. Maybe the pattern says, “I am unworthy to be loved or nothing ever works out for me.” This validates an ***abandonment wound*** and thickens the trauma bond as you feel responsible for maintaining their emotional stability. Verbally complaining or raging may be a toxic form of self-regulation. Most emotions are exaggerated. The good and the bad.

True love is free to come and free to go. You are free to say yes or free to say no. You are free to grow and develop your own identity and this will not threaten an emotionally healthy person. The best relationships grow trust over time at a steady pace. They are free to share feelings and misunderstandings and be heard and validated. Disagreements are resolved quickly.

Toxic relationships overshare too quickly, and past vulnerabilities and insecurities are identified. This may be innocent natural progression to develop connectedness. Or this may be a gathering of information to mimic your needs and move into a position of a confidant or trusted friend. *Oversharing* can be bullets to destroy you in a toxic breakup.

Exercise

History Evaluation: Spotting a Player?	
First, look at their patterns over the last ten years.	
1) Their past irresponsibility is high.	
2) Excuse making and blaming others are second.	
3) Dominance and control in relationships are common.	
4) Volatile breakups and domestic violence history.	
5) Relationships move too fast and are uncontrollable.	
6) Goal is to dominate thinking and behaviors.	
7) They prey on the innocent or the easy.	
8) They mimic your behaviors by listening carefully to what you need physically or emotionally and provide it.	
9) They learn your unmet needs and provide them.	
10) They learn your past wounds and exploit them.	
11) They make themselves indispensable.	
12) They are performers at the beginning. Giving you gratitude, adoration, and compliments.	
13) They obsess. You obsess. The relationship is intense.	
14) If they can't have you, they don't want anyone else to have you either. Intense possessiveness isn't love; it is possessiveness.	
15) They may try to invoke sympathy by describing their victimization in other relationships. This behavior will develop a tight ***negative bond of offense*** with others when they are later offended with you.	

16) Past relationships ended in disaster and not amicable.	
17) Co-dependency is extremely high.	
18) Self-destructive behaviors are common after break-up.	
19) Lack of conscience may be present.	
20) Lying is common.	
21) Their mood swings quickly…	
22) They cut you off from your friends.	
23) They entangle themselves financially: getting you to co-sign loans, using your credit cards for emergencies, convincing you to take out loans or student loans, sign a lease together, and they want to cohabitate too quickly.	
24) If the relationship is coming to an end, they blow up, bully you, or even threaten violence. Then establish themselves as a victim and you as the bully, so they can repeat the cycle with someone else. And, of course, assume no responsibility for the fall out.	
25) They may bully to back you down and then blame you or another. They triangulate others to push you into a corner to get their way.	
26) Boundaries threaten their sense of control and make them emotionally unstable. And then you get blamed for hurting them.	
27) They flip your words and try to say you made promises to them when you were speaking future dreams and visions with conditions of healthy relationship growth.	

A player may have many cyclical relationship addiction patterns but be totally unaware of their behavioral toxicity. They are insecure and always look to connect to someone to make them feel secure and safe. Then their dysfunctional behaviors emerge to control the relationship. But the insecurity is inside of them. **So, no matter how secure the relationship is they will always feel insecure and likely sabotage the relationship to repeat new relationships with the same addictive patterns.** If there is a choice between two partners, they will choose the weaker one they can control.

This player will talk about old wounds and past relationship failures and share problems for sympathy. If you listen to their words carefully you will be able to identify their motives in the relationship. Often, they are very wounded and broken inside. The lie may be that if they find the perfect someone that this lover will magically solve all their inner brokenness. The player has a load of *emotional unresolved baggage.* They always feel that half of themselves is missing. This is their individuality or identity that didn't get to form in adolescence.

Now if the player realizes you aren't fulfilling the empty half, they want to sabotage the relationship but make it your fault. They will argue or even rage and make it your fault so they can leave looking full of self-pity as a victim which will justify their continued self-destructive behaviors.

They may become emotionally unstable, impulsive, and lack self-control. There may be so much chaos that you give them half of everything you own to get a divorce or regain peace. They typically repeat their lies louder and louder to force you and others to believe them.

Players often believe and rehearse many self-defeating prophesies. "The rug will always be pulled out from under me." "Nothing I ever do will succeed."

If they bond securely and start to heal, they will not know how to sustain a healthy relationship without significant insight into old wounds, poor behavioral patterns and identification of their triggers and trauma wounds. They will need to intentionally learn to respond to difficulties with character and strength. (See the Rock of Recovery Overcoming Trauma Book.)

Behaviors of a player
1. Sensual
2. Romantic
3. Lots of kisses
4. Words of affirmation, affection, validation
5. Doting, caressing
6. Excitement
7. Sexual innuendos
8. Very present in the moment.

The Player's List to work in recovery:

1. They are hunters and need fuel for their ego.

2. They are bored with their current situation.
3. They love themselves.
4. They struggle with commitment.
5. They obsess and have difficulty stopping.
6. They have poor boundaries with themselves and others.
7. They have an addictive personality.
8. They have childhood trauma.

Are you Dealing with a Player?	
1) Verbally affectionate, uses flattery, and compliments.	
2) Notices little things about your appearance.	
3) Notices new clothes.	
4) Easily communicates their fast-growing feelings.	
5) Lusting after you. Obsessing. "I can't stop thinking about you."	
6) Talking sex. Enticing you with little gifts, flowers, or acts of service.	
7) Admiring you with their eyes.	
8) Wanting to touch and hold you without commitment.	
9) Listen to their words: Do they match their actions? "I don't love you like that." "I don't know what I want?"	

10) Feeling guilt, shame, or some other conflict when they are with you. Feeling one thing and saying something else.	
11) Backs you in a corner often. Maneuvers to get you alone.	
12) Grabs you inappropriately.	
13) Ignores your boundaries. Tells you how you feel.	
14) Jealous and wants to control you.	
15) Tracks your location or movements. Where are you at now? Where are you going? What are you doing? Who are you with?	
16) Past unstable relationships	
17) Blames others for past and current relationship failures.	
18) Plays the victim and then the bully.	
19) Plays the bully and then the victim.	

You can be a player or attract a player. A player is attracted to an empath who forgives easily and is vulnerable from past broken relationships and will make lots of excuses for poor behavior. An empath is easily sucked back in with a little love bombing and a few hours of nurturing and then the cycle of consuming and devaluing starts again. If you have been trapped in a repetitive cycle of drama, learn the signals of a player and the reasons for infidelity. Stop wiping the slate clean with forgiveness and demand relationship addiction recovery.

Truth of a player

A former player may be doing well in recovery and have goals and be establishing structure and safety in their life. They may be intentionally changing and growing… until a new relationship starts. This new relationship becomes their source. If they do a *focal shift* from healing internally to controlling the new person, recovery will become illusive quickly. This is a habitual pattern of stumbling and leads to *self-sabotage* which destroys everything good they just built.

When they find someone new, they cling quickly. The deception is that this new person will complete their identity and heal them. But when reality doesn't meet with the fantasy of a happy relationship, an old trauma or abandonment wound is easily triggered, and they give up on themselves and relapse with infidelity or other relationship destructive behaviors.

Inner core healing targets

- Insecure and lacking confidence.
- Broken internally and looking for someone to fix them.
- May have been molested as a child or have unresolved sexual trauma.
- Multiple other childhood traumas.
- Selfish or giving only for gain.

- Their ways move and are not dependable.
- They are divided internally into multiple immature parts that need healing. (See Rock of Recovery Spirit and Soul Disconnect Book.)
- They can't stop themselves and don't know their broken relationship patterns.
- They repeat toxic thinking patterns.
- They have no good boundaries with their emotions or thinking.
- Fake confidence. They develop a *fake self*. Often, they compromise their **core beliefs** to be accepted.
- Emotionally broken and unavailable.
- They usually weren't nurtured as children and didn't have a safe place to develop a strong identity.
- Survival skills were essential in a toxic environment in childhood.

Application

Learn to identify instability within yourself and others. Identify your non-negotiable goals for a true lover. Let your identification of sick behaviors motivate you to establish the groundwork for healthy relationships.

A true dream lover

- Emotionally available.

- Faithful.
- Present.
- Allows interdependency.

Principle

True love is never dominance, control, or manipulation.

Conclusion

If you know you are a player and you have hurt a dozen people and relapsed a dozen times, this is your pattern of suffering. Part of it isn't your fault, you never healed from past traumas and have developed deep and severe inner core wounds. Your recovery work must be intense and with strong accountability and with abstinence from any romantic relationships until you are much stronger.

Now, if you repeatedly attract toxic dominance in relationships, you may be severely wounded and too eager for attention. Work on your connection to safe people in safe places with strong accountability. You are not allowed to date anyone you haven't known for 6-12 months and who doesn't have the approval of your accountability group. It is likely that you don't value yourself and don't know your worth.

Observe the relationship patterns of potential partners. The lie is that there is only one opportunity for you to connect with your future partner or will lose the spontaneity, the magical connection, and your one true soul mate. Well, that's a lie.

If this person belongs to you, they won't be distracted with a new relationship several times a year. They will be working on their own maturity and waiting patiently for the right person to come along. They will treat you with respect and wait for you to be ready to begin a friendship. Development of a friendship over a period of 3-6 months is healthy and establishes trust. This would give you lots of space to determine if this person is a suitable match for your personality.

Remember casual sex is dangerous with long-term consequences and no control of who will get hurt or the outcome. You may end up with children by this person or marry a person because of a sexual connection that you never really liked just because you don't want to hurt their feelings or because you haven't dealt with your *rescuer mentality*. Premature sexual connection early in a relationship interrupts secure connection and develops fear bonds and not secure trust bonds.

When you become interested in someone, ask yourself would I want this person in my life for the next fifty years? Would I want to marry this person? If the answer is no, then for goodness' sake, don't go on a date with them.

Immaturity creates impulsivity and ends with a lifetime of consequences for poor decisions.

Lord, open my eyes to discern what is good for me. Help me to slow down enough that I can hear your directions. Let me see your warnings clearly. Help me to pause when I am confused or anxious. Then give me the power to make the best decision for my future. Give me the self-control to make wise, healthy, and mature choices. Help me to acknowledge my past relationship failures and identify the healing work I need to do. Amen.

LESSON 13

GROOMER

I cannot love another until I can love myself.

Introduction

Compared to a player who is driven by insecurity, a *groomer* knows exactly what they are doing and is *driven by self-absorption*. They are meticulous in their behaviors and controlled in their emotions and exhibit perfect character to win you over. They are setting a trap and covering their tracks.

Even if they become engaged to be married to you, the game may be to empty your bank accounts or embezzle resources for their new business. It is difficult to spot them through behaviors or words. These things are planned carefully and thoroughly. It will be their references from others, warnings from friends and family that will help you escape this relationship.

Lesson

Groomer	
1) A groomer will study you patiently.	
2) Develop a friendship and exhibit trustworthy behaviors.	
3) There is a history of grooming others to take advantage or rob without suspicion.	
4) There may have a past criminal history but talk often about their behavioral changes.	
5) They make themselves indispensable.	
6) They slowly gain control over things.	
7) They are very loyal and earn your devotion.	
8) They typically move slowly and methodically in earning your trust.	
9) They build their victim backstory and make it your idea to rescue them.	
10) They are often sincere.	
11) They are devious and cunning.	
12) They may take months or years to gain access to private, secure information.	
13) They may have a marvelous dream and need an investor.	

14) They act like you owe them something for their fake persona.	
15) They don't like being challenged. You will be called ungrateful.	

Wounded Prey

If you are wounded, vulnerable, broken and meet a groomer, beware you don't believe everything they say. They will speak with the tongue of a lover. The very one you longed for. They will do and say everything you wanted the one you loved to say and do. They will romance you and use words like charms. "You take my breath away." "I can't stop thinking about you." "You are so beautiful." *Their flattery is intoxicating.*

Oh, and if you are wounded, you may be the carefree player in this relationship. Two emotionally wounded and regressed people will be destruction to one another. If you are in recovery, you are both likely to relapse with the toxicity.

A player may be so wounded that they may or may not know what they are doing. But a groomer is usually calculating and precise with their actions. They know they don't love you. They may become fond of you later. You may fall deeply in love with their fake personification while they are romancing you. They want you but for their pleasure, or your ability to meet their needs.

Here are some warning signs:

A Groomer will not:

1. Commit to you.
2. Live for you or be willing to die for you, it's about their needs.
3. They know all along how to groom you and what to say. They have done it a dozen times.
4. It never crosses their mind to change their life for you. You were just in their path and willing.
5. They know how to make you feel loved, seen, cherished, doted on, embraced, and fulfilled.
6. A groomer is skilled in love bombing and makes you feel alive.
    a. Well, it's their special skill set. They are a con.
    b. They can con the money out of any old lady.
    c. And charm the unsuspecting.
    d. They are used to getting their way and making it happen and not taking no for an answer.
    e. A big dreamer.

So, here are your instructions. Do the *history evaluation* and then see the player/con/manipulator when you look into their eyes. Now identify any pretending. <u>Resistance will escalate the love bombing.</u> They are divided internally. There is a lover in them that adores you. But that part is not big enough to be real. They won't allow themselves to risk it all. They don't love you enough to move heaven and earth to be with you.

So, guard your heart with all diligence for out of it are the issues of life. Proverbs 4:23 Guard yourself. Make them be faithful. In this scenario: *A hook is their charm, and the bait is your naivety, loneliness, or brokenness.* The chink was the dream of the fairytale and need for attention. If you want this partner, you may get them. But reality would be much different than the romantic pursuer.

Exercise

Now write the character defects you see. These will escalate over time. Write a list of red flags.

Write out your friends' warnings and go slow.

If you are making a hundred excuses for poor behavior, you are the problem! Listen for those excuses and write them here:

Poor character emerges as soon as you set up expectations and require maturity. Also, when they have you on the hook the love-bombing intense phase will take too much energy to sustain, and they will start to complain. Afterall, it was the lure. It was fake. It wasn't real. It was a game.

The wounds of the past will be triggered in toxic relationships: rejection, abandonment, neglect, insecurity, feeling used, avoided, not validated, or nurtured and protected. Other wounds that will attract a toxic relationship are guilt, shame, self-condemnation, self-pity, along with feelings of being lonely, unwanted, unloved, too empathetic, people-pleasing, too giving and forgiving, vulnerable, and fairytale mentality.

Correct yourself and balance your expectations. Start relationships slowly.

Vulnerability: Needing to be loved. Feeling lonely, empty and with a void in your heart. You have old wounds that haven't healed and are looking for validation from an outside source. It is you that must love you and learn to nurture and care for you and make the best long-term decisions for yourself.

Compromise: Are you making up your own reality? Are you willing to compromise truth for a feeling?

Learned Patterns of Behavior

The Flirt becomes Easy Prey
Children of abuse often develop attention seeking behaviors:
1. Needy.
2. Likes to be center of attention.
3. Already confused in relationships
4. Unresolved emotional wounds
5. Easy prey because of belief in the fairytale.
6. Victim mentality
7. Not secure in their own identity
8. Looking for prince charming
9. Flirty and sensual
10. Lustful and Idolatrous
11. Unable to feel connected without sex.
12. Thinking that she can give more, and he will love more. This isn't true. The fallout will just be bigger.
Root issue: Hurting from a broken relationship that caused a wounded heart. Heal your inner brokenness. Grieve, forgive, and let go.

The vibrational pull of lust may make you drunk with pseudo-romance. It cannot be sustained.

Pseudo-love

This feels like love because it is intense but isn't love. It has a rocky Hollywood movie romance with the perfect ending feeling. It is pseudo-love to answer an obsession. It is a flesh driven charmer. You, friend, may be fooled. A groomer is a master manipulator.

Naïve, simple, unprotected, wounded, burdened, alone, vulnerable and the wolf in sheep's clothing moves in. Listen for their subtle motives. Long term toxic relationships will be a lifetime of suffering and will have very little structure, stability, security, or support. The toxicity will far outweigh the benefits. Co-parenting in this toxicity will be a nightmare.

Painful Relationship

It is possible that your marriage or steady relationship has been so painful that anything or anyone who gives you carefree love and attention helps you detach from the pain.

Maybe being playful and joyous is uncontrollable because it stops grieving. New relationships cannot be sustained until we grieve and heal the abandonment, rejection, neglect wounds of past relationships.

Broken Mentality

Immaturity will give it all just to be loved for a few moments. It's sad how an empty heart will compromise.

How far from Egypt we have come with you Lord, to circle around the wilderness and return to bondage and wait for rescue that we already had in our possession. If we only believe and pursued your promises.

The task master's rule isn't love. Well, not love for you. It is a desire to consume and walk away with their divided heart of self-absorption. How do you know they are self-absorbed? Everything is about them. They are never content.

Filthy like a beast.

Enamored with beauty but incapable of love. They will conform for appearance's sake. They know the words to say. The looks to give, the enticements of speech, the flattery, the kindness. *Many will follow their sensuality and will bring the way of truth into disrepute. 2 Peter 2:2*

Toxic Shame

Self-bondage is self-imposed shame, guilt, and self-condemnation for past indiscretions. This is called *toxic-shame* and has a harsh internal critic. This over responsible critic will do half the work of blaming themselves before the blame shifter starts their irresponsible behaviors. Because toxic shame needs a distraction, the groomer may be perfect. Excuse making for a bad day may be rehearsed for way too long as one bad day because a bad year.

Attracted to Abuse

Think about it, don't be stupid. Shut your heart off. Withdraw, hide, put up walls, see manipulator written on their palm. Player written on his forehead. Groomer enjoying the hunt.

If you come from an abusive family, you likely are attracting these types of narcissistic abusers and are just jumping ditches from one broken relationship to the next. Same game: different face, name, and place. Fatally attracted to one who vibrationally matches past abuse but is still *emotionally unavailable and unable to love.* This is called *compulsive repetition or re-enactment.*

Application

Maneater/Womanizer aka Cannibal

1) They may attract an unsuspecting person. This is exciting. They desire them to meet their needs, fulfill their lust.
2) They want and need admiration and attention.
3) They draw others towards them with flirting.
4) They love the chase.
5) If one pulls back, the other moves in. A real cat and mouse game. This is called *push-p*ull and is a behavior of insecure attachments.
6) Brokenness attracts a volatile person with instability.

7) This is fire and all consuming. It takes over the thought life.
8) Cannibals are flesh-eaters and are about the chase or the hunt, and the conquest. Under perfect circumstances it could be about love and devotion, but usually ends up being about intense lust and passion with verbal abuse and even violence.
9) This devourer doesn't even know their patterns or their power.
10) Once they have conquered, they devalue and blame the other to establish a rationalization for their discarding the relationship.
This unintentional sabotage is because of the fear of relationships or trauma bonds and don't know what they want and do not have the internal reflection to study themselves or the character to sustain growth and healing.
Result: Confusion, wounded hearts, and broken lives on both sides. It is difficult to not desire to return and repeat the cycle to resolve the confusion. If cycle is repeated, this will give momentary relief with the make-up sex and love-bombing but eventually will cause more destruction and confusion.

METHODOLOGY TO FIND VICTIMS

Warning: Any toxic person who isn't interested in recovering find enablers to help them stay sick. Prepare yourself. It is important to understand that you will receive resistance and be told you are paranoid. This resistance can escalate into toxic verbal or even physical abuse quickly. If this happens, let it increase your determination to pursue healthier relationships. Push back and maintain your right to a peaceful life.

These are classic methods to observe and proceed cautiously:

1) Catchy pick-up lines at the grocery store, gas station, new employment, night club, strip club, drug/alcohol rehabilitation centers, recovery meetings, etc.
2) Passionate and energetic with lots of dreams and goals.
3) Flatters and boast in their speech
4) Moves fast in relationships especially with sexual intimacy.
5) Quickly entangles you financially (within months) • Borrows money with promise to repay. • Many promises of future financial windfall: inheritance, workers' compensation claim, lawsuits, etc. *This is a lottery mentality.* • Coaches you on how to get student loans, credit cards, etc.

• Coaches you on how to use emotional manipulation to embezzle money from unsuspecting loved ones.
6) Pretends helplessness: Then lavishes praise for meeting their desperate needs. They are temporarily down on their luck. You are the angel to rescue them from despair. • Needs a place to do laundry. • Needs a couch to sleep on a few nights. • Needs a phone for potential employers to call. • Needs new shoes and clothes for job interview
7) Plays the victim like a champion. • Replays old wounds. • Recants martyrdom and unselfish acts that weren't appreciated
8) Finds common ground with you and may charm your family • **A chameleon**- They can gauge a situation and temporarily change their behavior and become the perfect companion, stepparent, cook, housekeeper, etc. • Takes on the persona of whoever they are around and becomes who others want them to be. • Deludes significant others that could protect you. • Slurs family and friends that are warning you or are suspicious of them. • Separates you from anyone who isn't fooled by them and who could protect you.

Any good behavior is temporary. Challenge it.

Does the good behaviors disappear when you…

- Question them.
- Don't play the game.
- Set a boundary.

AVOIDING PITFALLS

Test new relationships:

- Go slow.
- Set up accountability and expectations.
- Turn their recovery over to stronger people that can hold them accountable if they have a history of substance use disorder or domestic violence (support groups, sponsors, counselors, etc.)
- Expect 3-5 years of solid recovery and employment before considering a serious relationship with them.
- Question past behaviors
- Ask them to acknowledge their shortcomings.
- Don't rescue them from consequences of previous poor choices.
- Ask other people about their history.
- Expect other adults to be responsible for their own financial needs.
- Talk to their ex-mates or ex-lovers.

- Don't overlook lies and early betrayals.
- Set firm boundaries.

Honeymoon Phase

Love bombing can lead to healthy relationships and be more like a normal honeymoon phase. This type of love bombing is enjoyed by both partners who has the capacity to love and the character to be loyal and maintain the relationship. If both partners are mature, they can enjoy each other's company and move forward easily in life if the relationship ends.

Toxic Love-bombing

If love bombing is immature and meant to fulfill an addictive need for attention, self-fulfillment, and ego supply this relationship will probably not end well.

The partners will become codependent, make excuses for poor behaviors, and tolerate a significant amount of abuse after the initial phase of the relationship is over attempting to reconnect with the initial intensity.

This relationship can become toxic fast. One partner may genuinely care about the other. The other may be controlling and vacillate between being a bully and playing a victim.

Review Potential Toxicity
1. Early intense Love-bombing characteristics

2. Moving too fast
3. Deep conversations and oversharing
4. Excessive texting and calling
5. Embraces, kisses, hugs that makes you feel seen, heard, and validated.
6. There may be intensity in the relationship. This may feel like a viable life partner one moment and a bad divorce the next.
7. The person may give all their love and attention and retreat and be minimally connected.
8. Push-pull behaviors are common. Come here. Go away.
9. Characterized by confusion.
10. Intense jealousy is common.
11. They may already be in a committed relationship.

Potential Toxic Addictive Qualities
1. Intermittently hot and cold; push-pull behaviors.
2. Hyperventilating anxiety with absence of connectedness with the lack of ability to self-regulate.
3. Obsessing over each other.
4. Lustful thinking. Fantasy relationship with role playing where you can control what the other says and does. This fantasy thinking isn't reality.
5. Super sensitive to over analyze everything.

6. Losing your identity and altering your entire life too quickly
7. Exaggerated emotions; easily offended

Principle

I cannot love another until I can love myself.

Conclusion

Addicted Brain

Know that if you are driven like a dog and cannot stop yourself, it isn't real. It won't last. It is just another addiction. Sex …the chase…the game… will just feed your addicted brain. Often, you hate the person more afterwards, than you ever loved them to begin with.

Lord, help me to love me. Help me to value myself and to elevate my standard of thinking of myself. Let me not settle for abuse or toxicity. Let me take back my power. Let me grow and mature in a way that I can give and receive true love. Give me discernment that I may see the heart of others and enough self-control to choose what is right for me and my future. Amen.

LESSON 14

SEXUAL TRAUMA AND BEHAVIOR RESPONSES

Healthy love lets us come and go and rejoices in our individuality.

INTRODUCTION

Evaluate your past sexual traumas. Develop a strong sense of yourself. Ask: where do I begin? Where do I end? How much of myself am I willing to invest in another person? If you haven't healed, do not start a relationship. It will be fraught with emotional chaos.

A lack of development around identity can produce a strong internal fantasy world. Anyone who crosses your path can become an obsession. This person will be included in your fantasy with your total control.

These relationships are pretend but feel real. This may be causes from mild dissociative patterns developed around childhood trauma. The traumas can range from neglect where you were left alone and attached to fictional characters from television or movies to repetitive childhood molestations where you detached from reality and developed a safe internal space.

This was a functional coping skill for a toxic environment for a child but is destructive for an adult. It will prevent you from developing healthy attachments.

If you pursue a person from your obsessive ruminating, limerent patterns, you have already done most of the work of forming a *fake trust bond* through *controlled fantasy*. The relationship will move too fast and won't be a safe place for you to grow and heal.

Lesson

Am I Sexually Traumatized?	
1) Am I lusting often?	
2) Do I fantasize often?	
3) Do I struggle with a porn addiction or an attachment to television, actors, musicians, or inanimate objects?	
4) Have I healed from my past sexual traumas?	
5) Do I know how to connect without sex?	
6) Do I often physically connect before a healthy	

spiritual connection is developed?	
7) Was I sexually molested as a child?	
8) If I was molested, how much trauma was it on a scale of 1-10, with 10 being extreme trauma? How old was I? (The age of your molestation/trauma is the developmental age you are stuck in when you get triggered.)	
9) Do I carry guilt, shame, and blame myself often for things I had no control over?	
10) Do I blame others excessively or can I own my part in adult relationships?	
11) Was my childhood home safe or violent?	
12) Was I called names and told I asked for the abuse?	
13) Was I threatened to keep silent?	
14) Do I feel violated or loved in relationships?	
15) Do I feel safe or unsafe?	
16) Was my entire childhood covered in lies and fear?	
17) Was I molested by family, stepfamily members or strangers?	
18) Do I have an aversion to sex?	
19) Was my last partner unfaithful?	
20) Do I have sexually transmitted diseases I need to address?	

21) Do I have betrayal, abandonment, neglect, abuse wounds that need healed?	
22) Do I start and stop relationships quickly?	
23) Do I obsess until I have someone locked into a relationship with me and then devalue and discard them?	
24) Do relationship failures cause me to relapse into substance use disorder or eating disorders?	
25) How many past abusive relationships have I been involved in?	
26) How many relationships am I in where I am an equal partner?	
27) Do I have a safe friend/sponsor/counselor to help expose the skeletons in my closet?	

Wounded people look for others to heal them but have not done the work to heal themselves. Instead, they attract people like the ones who wounded them. Our vibrational energy will likely draw people to us that are like those in our past. Subconsciously, relational patterns repeat themselves. We can be oblivious to this *repetitive compulsion*. We may just exchange a physical abuser for an emotional abuser.

We may unintentionally pick up wounded people to help them become stronger. This is done because of our *overcompensating caretaker role.* Plus, it may be the way we find value or worth is to choose someone who needs us. It also may be a way to distract us from doing the uncomfortable work to heal our own emotional pain.

Now decide, am I continually in the same broken place: different people, places, and names, but the same scenario? If so, stop and take 6-12 months to explore those wounds through counseling, support groups, reading books on the subject or watching lectures on YouTube on how to heal from the past. If you can name the problem, you can research it, educate yourself and progress towards healing.

Any life-threatening behavior patterns or traumatic emotional wounds should include sessions with a trained counselor. Childhood sexual trauma will take several years of counseling and diligent work to heal. Support groups and safe places are a vital way to navigate deep struggles.

Children of parents with substance use disorder or who grow up in domestic violence without being nurtured have abnormal views of relationships. Their sense of reality is skewed.

Children of narcissistic parents may be great performers but will always feel unloved. Children of physically and verbally abusive parents may develop people-pleasing behavior to validate their worth in a relationship. They may feel unworthy within themselves.

> *Skewed thinking is a learned pattern of survival.*

Often those who have been abused have very low expectations and settle for crumbs in a relationship. Others have a fairytale mentality and think healthy relationships are Hollywood with happy endings. Real relationships have struggles. We grow and mature through these struggles, or we self-implode into the victims of circumstance.

A *survival mentality* can develop flesh-eating piranha or devouring behaviors to temporarily meet our needs. This ends in a *power game of self-protection* with no real connection.

Children of narcissistic parents may have been their parent's ego supply but were not nurtured, did not form their own identity, and became commodities to be exploited within the family. This stunted their emotionally development into survival skills to extract attention from others but are fearful of connection and will often sabotage relationships quickly.

Am I a Piranha?	
1) Do I have push-pull tendencies?	
2) Do I know what I want in a relationship and then I change?	
3) Do I flirt even if I am in a committed relationship?	
4) Do I like to play the field and keep my options open?	
5) Do I like to have casual sex?	
6) Do I lie or exaggerate often?	
7) Do I have a conscious?	
8) Do I care if I hurt another?	
9) Am I obsessed with and pursuing another I don't really want?	
10) Do I like to be the center of attention?	

11) Do I want the power to attract a person away from another to validate myself?	
12) Do I make promises I won't likely keep?	
13) I am looking for a fairytale?	
14) Do I like to pretend to be someone I am not?	
15) Do I like to create drama?	
16) Do I have a string of broken relationships behind me?	
17) Do I sabotage my relationships intentionally?	
18) Do I have a history of being unfaithful?	
19) Do I have grandiose self-absorption tendencies?	
20) Am I attracted to a people who make me crazy?	
21) Do I want them until I get them and then despise them?	
22) Do I often chew up others and spit them out?	
23) Am I impulsive?	
24) Am I ignoring the obvious past actions and behaviors of this person and have magical thinking that this time will be different?	
25) Am I emotionally unavailable and refuse to commit?	
26) Do I panic when someone gets close to me and sabotage the relationship?	
27)Do I feel unstable and am looking for someone else to complete me?	

When toxic relationships are my norm, I may be a piranha.

Piranhas are flesh eaters and devour others. They have no identity of their own and strip another of theirs to fill that void. Because of their selfishness, the person devoured may lose their life in addictive patterns of destruction. **This is not a game!**

Exercise

Evaluate any false thinking or behaviors.

Application

Fantasy vs Emotionally Unavailable lovers

Fantasy Relationship-totally controllable in your imagination. In a real relationship, previous fantasy highlights the good stuff. The bad stuff is forgotten or glossed over. This is called *romanticizing*. There is a deep discontent in any new relationships that does not meet the expectations of the fantasy which develops instability.

Unavailable lover-A player on the hunt. This lover usually does not intend to connect emotionally. They do not know how. They are usually wounded and go from one broken relationship to another. They only want the relationship that they cannot have or one of convenience to meet their needs.

The Fantasy Relationship
1. Available

2. Convenient
3. Controlled
4. Rooted in old wounds and feelings of helplessness.
5. New relationships are quickly ruined by:
• Imaginary perfection of the fantasy relationship
• Romanticizing a past toxic relationship (forgetting the toxic parts and remembering the good).
• Unable to fully trust another person.
• Unable to be content in relationships.
• Unable to be faithful.
• A Grand Canyon of emptiness INTERNALLY that even 100 lovers could not fill.
Making your new partner live under the shadow of the imaginary perfect lover is common.
Root Issue: There were no healthy relationship models growing up. There is no ability to recognize healthy love.

Emotionally Unavailable
1. Bored
2. Easily distracted.
3. Attention seeker.
4. Relationship addict
5. Non-committal

6. Broken and confused vs Devouring Man-eater/Womanizer
7. Let others choose them, easily gives themselves sexually.
8. Easily enticed.
9. Gets involved with partners they would never want to spend their life connected to.
10. Careless in relationships
11. Lack of emotional availability…overly emotional then emotionally shut down.
12. Their ways are moveable.
13. This relationship is like trying to hold the wind.
Root Issue: *Neither of these people love themselves, so they can't fully be available and love another in a safe connection. They do not possess a healthy sense of themselves.*

Principle

Healthy love lets us come and go and rejoices in our individuality.

Conclusion

If I haven't done the work to heal internally, no relationship will be healthy. If my level of trust in myself is low, trust in another will also be low.

If I am suspicious and paranoid of past lovers, new lovers will evoke the same responses. If I take the time to do my healing and find several non-sexual relationships I can enjoy, I can learn what I like and don't like in a safe space.

I can develop my own identity. This should have been done in childhood and through my teenage years, but trauma may have me stuck in a perpetual childlike state of emotional immaturity.

Building my own identity will help me develop healthy self-esteem. Then, I can maturely and patiently decide what kind of a partner I would enjoy.

Then I can intentionally pursue relationships as I have the healing and self-control to nurture myself first. If I can do what is best for me and learn the *skill of contentment*. Then I will be free to find love. I won't need to control others. I won't need to manage their lives and fix them. I won't need to hide parts of myself. I can enjoy healthy sharing, good communication and building a healthy connection.

Lord, I thank you that I felt loved and connected for a moment. I thank you that I can recognize my toxic patterns and the patterns of the people I choose or attract. Thank you for ending poor relationships and protecting me. Help me to recognize when it is real and when it is just a feeling. Help me know who I am and who I am not. Let me establish awareness that my internal brokenness will make me emotionally unavailable to everyone in my life. Help me to start small and allow myself to be emotionally available to a few in my life. Show me safe people. Let me learn to safely connect. Amen.

CHAPTER 15

INFIDELITY & REPAIR

Infidelity is reckless and will contaminate your life.

Introduction

Infidelity in relationships is common. We may not have developed a mature conscience. There may be a lack of commitment. There may be multiple past partners with betrayal wounds that haven't healed. It may be that you feel trapped in an abusive relationship but are incapable of leaving for various reasons. An extra marital affair may be a toxic coping strategy.

You likely feel stagnant and have lost your way and have let your guard down and are distracted from your life goals. Afterall, this will keep you from having to deal with the problems in your current relationship or the changes you need to make in yourself to heal. Your focus may be on your wounded heart which causes you an inordinate amount of self-absorption. An affair will only be a distraction from your current state of suffering. It makes more problems and escalate old problems.

Lesson

Without a healthy identity you will develop a *fake self.* This pseudo-self will be whatever you think another wants you to be. A toxic marriage will rob you of your identity and make you vulnerable to be reshaped into a new person you don't recognize.

This new romance releases hormones and chemicals in the brain that elevates your mood and alleviates depression and may give you some sense of yourself through the movement of deciding. Even though this decision is toxic, it gives you a sense of control that you probably have lost in other areas of your life.

Infidelity is a reckless game. Most are not normally cunning and deceptive enough to navigate such behaviors and compartmentalize them and return to their significant other as if nothing has happened. It will contaminate all areas of your life.

Infidelity changes your personality. If you have been a doormat for years, stuck in an abusive situation, ignored or invisible in a painful relationship, it may give you the courage to push back and divorce. Or the fallout from adultery can force you to face your marital issues, give you the strength to change and heal the brokenness in your family. You may realize your marriage/family is worth saving.

Adultery can create a crisis to propel you forward if you have been stuck for years. It is a symptom of a much deeper problem. Find the root issues.

Adultery is a stupid choice and will hurt many, yourself included. Sexual relations without commitment always have unforeseen, uncontrollable consequences. Many will be hurt. This fore knowledge is not usually powerful enough to stop the new relationship if you are intensely wounded or have deep rejection wounds from others. You may be in total denial of your vulnerability until you are knee deep into some impossible magical fairytale ending. There are no guardrails in an affair. There is no safety net to catch you. Devastation is around the curve.

So, if your current relationship is stuck, you lack the skills to work on yourself, radically accept your partner and be content or leave for your sanity and get help, you are extremely vulnerable. These wounds or cracks in your thinking cause poor boundaries that usually attract a new relationship with a myriad of its own toxicity. You are not secure enough in your own identity to choose a healthy partner. Wait and work on yourself. Now let's look at some risk factors that need addressed as soon as possible.

Risk factors for an affair
1. Chronic grieving over losses.
2. Love Starved
3. Denied intimacy in marriage.

4. Abusive partner
5. Avoidant partner

The best option would be to remove yourself from the environment of the person who is the object of your attraction. In six months, you both will be single and free to date or thrilled you escape near disaster.

If you do not have an addictive personality or pornography issues and have viewed sex in a wholesome way this chapter will make no sense to you. But, if you were molested as a child, dealt with sexual perversion in your family, and was introduced to porn at a young age, there will be a battle to be fought that may take half your life to win if you start now. If you also live in domestic violence, have substance use disorder and obsessive thinking patterns, prepare yourself with a community that understands sexual trauma issues.

Healthy love lets you come and go and rejoices in your individuality. It learns to develop secure connection and yet retains individuality. It builds trust bonds and not fear bonds.

Trust bond is shared intimacy of your daily feelings, and your physical, emotional, and spiritual needs are heard and being met. Comfort is always at your front door from yourself and your trusted others. You will learn to *confidently strengthen yourself* when no one else is available when you build a trust bond with yourself. Many of us, do not trust ourselves to love ourselves.

Trust sets you on a safe pathway to explore old wounds, release them, change your thinking and behaviors. Trust opens your heart to listen closely to yourself and others. Trust is soft and gentle, easy to entreat and easy to forgive another. Then, you will have no reason to follow a toxic attraction for another. You will be content in a healthy and fulfilling relationship, even if this relationship is only with yourself. Finding contentment is key for mental health.

A *fear bond* is controlling, dominant, and even pouty when it doesn't get its way. The fear bond blocks your heart from trusting another or receiving love or comfort. It sets you on a path to destroy your relationships and you feel deep loneliness without resources to find any peace. The goal is survival and self-preservation. You consume and consume some more and can never be satisfied.

Fear blocks healthy connection. It sabotages any successful relationship with emotional instability. This develops into hardness of heart and intense stubbornness often with an exhibition of anger, depression, or self-destructive behaviors.

Fear builds a fortress of solitude where no one can have any piece of your heart or ever hurt you again, hence, survival is the theme. Find the hardest, most difficult, angriest person you know and realize they are a hurt wounded soul without the skills to connect because they never learned to trust.

Fear bonds are formed as protection so no one will ever get to know you. Your *harsh internal critic* makes you feel unlovable, and you hide your *true self* from others with the thinking that if they really knew you, they wouldn't love you. This root problem is that you don't love yourself. **To heal, you must learn to love you**.

To stop your pattern of going from one broken relationship to another, you must slow down and learn to love and accept your own self. Then you must find safe people and safe places to build a community of friends. Will you get hurt again? Of course, you will, but no matter, now the wall of love for yourself will protect your heart and give you compassion for another. This will help you to see their wounded heart and how they are deflecting their pain on you. This rejection will not be your identity. Your new identity will be a love for yourself and for others.

If you heal, you will not give others the power to deeply wound you. Nor will you hold bitterness and let it rob you of your peace. You will be able to hold your love for yourself and your peace because you will know your worth and eternal value. You will be a stable anchor in the storm for others to return to when they are ready to do their own work.

So, is your current relationship so sick and you are too much of a coward to exit maturely? Instead, an affair would force the other person to confront you and maybe leave or it would give you momentary relief. The secret source of affection from an affair is a sick way to cope with your other miserable relationship and suffer through it. An affair is just a symptom of a broken relationship. It isn't the root issue.

If you are severely wounded with abandonment, rejection issues and other trauma wounds, you are incredibly vulnerable to attract a devourer. The intense attraction that you feel isn't love, it is a trauma bond. You will know it is a trauma bond because you are overwhelmingly compelled and compulsively obsess over this person. This is volatile and could end in severe destruction with public humiliation and even violence. If you can understand an intense attraction as the repetition compulsion of old trauma wound maybe you can educate yourself enough to not act on it.

Now it's important to evaluate the reasons adultery was able to infiltrate your marriage/relationship.

Exercise

Explore the Reasons you have or might want to commit adultery.

A sick coping skill to deal with a dead or broken marriage is the lure of an affair. If you are in a committed relationship and thinking about having an affair, stop and process the reasons why you would entangle yourself in such a mess. If you were totally free, would you choose this new partner?

Reasons for Adultery	
1. Conscience is not fully developed or has been readjusted to fit the norm of today's society.	

2. Opportunity exists or is sought after.	
3. Physical attraction led to addictive obsession.	
4. Physical needs… one mate is ignoring, avoiding or unavailable.	
5. Emotional wound by your mate: unwanted, unloved, neglected, abandoned, rejected and you have lost yourself.	
6. Partner is unwilling or incapable to meet your needs.	
7. Partner is unsuited to your personality and has never understood your love language and doesn't even try.	
8. Adultery may give you the complete detachment that you need to get a divorce and find someone capable of loving you.	
9. You convince yourself that you are in love and that God wouldn't mind. You wouldn't be hurting anyone, no one will know. You can compartmentalize this and get away with it. This type of rationalization is a danger zone.	
10. Unaddressed past sexual addictions which cause obsessing, lusting and that cannot stop until you act on it.	
11. Adultery has been a life-time habit.	
12. Lack of empathy for how your partner will be affected by this act.	
13.Childhood trauma	
14.Intense unresolved anxiety	
15.History of Domestic Violence	
16.Untreated substance use disorder	

Fire belongs in the firepit. It is beautiful to look at and can roast your marshmallows. But once it is taken out of the firepit you cannot control whether it burns the whole forest or who will be trapped and consumed by the flames.

The Affair

So, you say you love her, the other woman?
Do you lay and cry for her?
Are you wanting to defend, protect, and comfort her?
Do you want to provide for her?
Do you just like the excitement she gives?
And the way she makes you feel?
Are you just bored?
Do you feel guilt and shame afterwards?
Do you even think about how it will affect others?
Do you even care?

Possible Root Issues
1. Not enough self-control.
2. Not enough character to develop a standard of fidelity in marriage.
3. Bored.
4. Looking for someone to be your savior, fix your problems, and fulfill your needs.
5. Discontentment with life in general.

6. So many past broken relationships that you don't even try to be faithful anymore.
7. Stuck and unable to decide to end your current relationship and this looks like movement.

Application

Repentance is a change in our thinking. A turning around 180 degrees. A movement towards healing. If past infidelity has you stuck and beating yourself up. This immaturity will land you in another toxic coping skill. It could cause you to relapse into substance use disorder or take your life. Instead, use it as a springboard to explore healing.

Don't Beat Yourself Up.

It is unreasonable to think that you wouldn't want a healthy, loving relationship. It may be momentarily medicating your suffering. If you have compromised and entered an affair or repeatedly settled for toxic relationships, work on yourself to figure out what is broken, and needs healed. Otherwise, you are just going to do this again. Might as well work on this now.

Affair Repentance

Discover your motives before confessing to your partner about the affair. Things to consider: Are you telling them to redeem the relationship and build a bond of trust? Are you telling them to cleanse your conscious? Are you telling them to make them suffer? Will this be helpful or hurtful?

Draw within yourself a space of solitude but not isolation. Set boundaries to protect yourself from such nonsense again. Thank God for the opportunity to identify your false thinking, selfish bent, trauma bonds, insecure attachments, or wounded spirit.

Infidelity Repentance **Repentance is a change in thinking.**	
1. Am I truly repentant or just sorry I got caught?	
2. Do I have a short and long-term plan for infidelity recovery?	
3. Am I dealing with the real problems or just the consequences?	
4. Do I have an accountability partner and a recovery group or counselor?	
5. Am I grieving over my lack of self-control and developing stronger character?	
6. Have I acknowledged responsibility for my poor choices?	
7. Am I hiding anything?	

8. Am I using the confusion as an opportunity to relapse into drug or alcohol addictions?	
9. Am I choosing healthy friends or isolating?	
10. Am I making restitution for past offenses?	
11. Have I established boundaries to prevent a relapse into infidelity?	
12. Am I serving others and giving back to family and community?	
13. Do I consistently repeat a cycle of infidelity/regret/relapse? If so, I need stronger boundaries and/or harder consequences. Was this my first indiscretion? Have I explored my thinking patterns that led to infidelity?	
14. Am I blaming my significant other's inattentiveness for my behaviors?	
15. Am I setting up an offense and triangulating and negatively bonding with others to justify my pity party when I am caught?	
16. Am I playing a victim and deflecting responsibility and projecting the other person in the affair as the only responsible party?	

> *When it comes to infidelity recovery, expect honesty and a desire to rebuild trust.*

Infidelity Recovery Accountability
1. Keep financial accounts open to the scrutiny of another who understands sexual addictions.
2. Keep all phone calls on speaker phone for others to hold you accountable.
3. No contact is best. A complete severance from all toxic relationships is best.
4. If I must have contact because of shared parenting, keep all visits short and with a trusted friend if possible.
5. With shared parenting. No physical or verbal contact for a specified period may be needed with a third-party transporting any children for visitations.

Principle

Infidelity is reckless and will contaminate your life.

Conclusion

When it's over

Lust never makes a healthy relationship. It lands in loss of yourself with lingering taste of poison. It blocks your path to peace and makes you crazy.

Lust lights a fire that is difficult to stop. It is sick and dysfunctional and can drive obsessive thinking. It feels like love. It feels like passion. It takes up way too much space in your life and produces suffering. But reality will eventually catch up with you. Lust isn't real. It will always disappoint.

The next chapters we will explore how to heal. It will take work to see the patterns and heal old wounds. It will take recovery to discover why you chose the path of infidelity. Were you careless? Bored? Wounded? Abandoned? Lustful? There are character flaws that need to be addressed and inner healing that needs done.

So, when it is over, and you are devastated make a grateful list. Take a thought of devastation when your romance ends and stretch it with gratefulness. Grateful for the experience. Grateful to be seen, heard, held, validated even if it was just for a moment. Even if it was immature, even if it ended in destruction. Grateful that you escaped. Grateful that you were protected, Grateful that you can come back to your senses and learn to find your safe inner-self.

Grateful List:

Navigate the emotions by extracting the lessons you learned from this experience. Find the emotional skills to move on. Expand your thinking. Make your thoughts elastic so you can move and shape your thoughts into a healthy learning experience.

Lessons Learned:

Lord, forgive me, help me to forgive myself and others. Purge me with hyssop, and I shall be clean; wash me, and I shall be whiter than snow. Let me hear joy and gladness; let the bones that you have broken rejoice. Hide your face from my sins and blot out all my iniquities. Create in me a clean heart, O God, and renew a right spirit within me. Restore to me the joy of your salvation and uphold me with a willing spirit. Psalm 51:7-12 Amen.

LESSON 16

CPTSD

Healing toxic thinking and relationship patterns makes space to develop healthy relationship skills.

Introduction

Childhood trauma trains us to accept crumbs in relationships. It teaches us to gaslight and betray ourselves. We tend to settle for very little attention and feel we are lucky to get it. We believe lies about ourselves and our circumstances so long that they have become our truth. If childhood trauma was intense, we develop complex post-traumatic stress disorder which causes dysfunctional adult relationships.

Accepting Crumbs

Have you allowed yourself to be second?
Have you settled for second best?
Does the empath in you want to take care of others?
Was the role of caretaker a survival skill as a child?
Does the victim in you give without expecting any reciprocation?
Is the adult-child in you very small?
Have you expected very little?
Have you compromised?
Have you blindly trusted?
Does even a scrap of attention feel like love?
Does the martyr in you cling strongly to abusive people?
Are you stuck in perpetual grieving?
This is sad!

Lesson

When a healthy identity does not form within us, we are always looking to another to validate and nurture the child inside of us. This lack of identity develops complex issues in relationships. Trauma bonding feels like love. Obsessive limerence feels like intense attraction. Control feels like protection. Dominance gives us a poverty-slave mentality. Abandonment and neglect make us rebellious and self-destructive, and we develop a negative internal critic and become stuck in a helpless syndrome. These patterns all keep us stuck.

We feel helpless and powerless to move forward. The dark places of depression become the only safe place we know. It is a place where no one can reach us, and no one can hurt us. We are just numb. The future looks bleak and every way we turn seems to be blocked with disappointment. We see from the lenses of trauma. To make the drastic changes and launch into an unknown future brings more anxiety than just giving up and staying stuck in the familiar.

Childhood trauma kept our brains from developing. We awake every morning with anxiety. We go to sleep with our bitterness. Our emotions drive our decisions and are immature and exaggerated. We learn to not trust anyone or anything.

As I have looked at CPTSD (complex post-traumatic stress disorder), I have learned enough to know that the connections in our brains didn't form correctly, and we can't think our way out of a situation.

How long have you struggled against a feeling? How long have you tried to make movement forward? How long have you tried to make sense out of a betrayal, a molestation, or an unjust beating? How much have you felt misunderstood, unseen, and unknown?

I tell you today; you cannot think your way through the mire of stupidity… just let it go. Learn these skills in the *Rock of Recovery Detachment book.*

You can think through a problem all your life and never find a resolution. Just let it go and move forward. As a child raised in trauma, you weren't safe and didn't form your own identity. You weren't safe to explore and develop your own personality. You had to conform and learn survival skills.

This means you don't have the brain connection to think problems through to a resolution. Your character was developed based on survival not on being nurtured and protected and with principles of truth.

Your emotions are immature and still very loud. As you work through the *Rock of Recovery Overcoming Trauma* book you will learn to recognize when you get triggered and purposefully respond differently and with the steady character of love, joy, and peace. You will grow in character and learn to trust yourself, develop your authentic self and love yourself.

It is possible that you don't feel connected or alive without a roller coaster relationship. There needs to be a discovery of the reasons you have been attracted to those who are toxic and cannot return love.

In a safe relationship, you may flip and become the abuser and continue the roller coaster emotions. The brain releases chemicals during these chaotic times. We may learn behavioral patterns of rage. Intense complaining and verbally berating our significant other may be a response to internal dysregulation and give us a false sense of control. Intense sadness or depressive feelings may paralyze us, and we want to sleep to avoid life. These become addictive emotional pattern.

Maybe you can't connect without sexual intimacy. And yet, you are incapable of choosing healthy partners. Trauma bonds cling, consume and suck the life out of you and feel impossible to break without more trauma.

This happens because you didn't develop your own identity. Therefore, you tend to take on the identity of another and attach insecurely. The relationship starts beautifully but is unsustainable because you have no identity and become quickly enmeshed in a trauma bond and devalue yourself and allow your identity to be shaped by this new relationship. Or you consume the other person and attempt to exert dominance and extreme control. Since you don't know who you are, this person becomes your other half and if they leave, you will not know who you are…again. This lack of your own self-worth, healthy identity and healthy boundaries is a set up for a relationship addiction.

Love Addiction

You can love and feel loved by them.
This love may be mostly in your head. But then,
You may be drawn to them more than you ever dreamed possible.
Every thought is on them.

They may be an irresistible magnet.
There may be 100 red flags you ignore.
Excuses may become your middle name.

A wounded soul is already low.
And may be enamored with the attention.
Powerless to stop. Powerless to say no.

Taking solace in your obsession.
Completely sincere. Completely insane.
Incapable of sustaining this level of vulnerability.

Your old fear bond triggered.
Emerging to destroy beauty.
An old abandonment wound hurling sabotage.

Those who come out of toxic relationships need a ban on dating for 1-2 years. Even potentially awesome relationships will be sabotaged by old wounds. Recognize your relationship patterns.

People in passive relationship recovery will regress to dysfunctional communication. Dysfunctional patterns of nuclear families will be evident. We are trained from childhood in how to respond to one another within the home. Our homes may have been violent, with constant arguing, and generally unpleasant. Blame shifting seems to be the weapon of choice used to validate their position of offense.

Most individuals, with a lack of identity and poor boundaries, when agitated will develop an arsenal of reasons to justify their offense and triangulate third-party individuals to side with them. Arrogance seeks out others who will listen to half of the story and agree with their judgment. This response has no possible healthy resolution. This causes deep wounds that keep repeating toxic relationship patterns. We literally force others to abandon us because of our toxic behaviors.

Exercise

Determine your relationship sabotage level.

Application

Relationship Sabotage

Passive Sabotage
1. Pouting
2. Slamming doors
3. Banging dishes
4. Silent treatment
5. Withdraw of affection
6. Playing the victim
7. Third party complaining
8. No eye-contact.
9. Refusal to communicate.
10. Making yourself sick
11. Sighing and eye rolling
12. Avoidance

Aggressive Sabotage
1. Conflict initiation over trivial things
2. Blame shifting
3. Intense slander
4. Complaining, griping, bickering
5. Must have the last word.
6. Refusal to own my part.
7. Raging with frustration.
8. Affairs
9. Relapse in Substance Use Disorder
10. Domestic Violence
11. Hiding all the money or reckless spending

These behaviors divide families for decades and set you up for relationship confusion.

Toxicity always races blindly around a curvy mountain with no guardrails.

Undealt with past relationship wounds will cause you to be reckless. You will not be able to trust your instincts and will not be able to choose a healthy person or securely attach. If you find a healthy relationship, you will sabotage it.

You may not even want to attach to anyone anymore. You may go into a relationship with the end in sight.

An oath to never love again is a deep wound from past brokenness and will set you up for a callous, isolated heart that is not only incapable of receiving love but makes you a hater. **Renounce the oaths you have made to never love again.** Start with learning to give yourself love and receive kindness and love from yourself to you.

Hater

Hate for a past lover.
An oath to never love again.
Unsafe to love.
Cynical.
Set up for toxicity.
Find your peace.

Recognize old relationship wounds. **Go back and own your part, forgive, and release your past partners.**

A Relationship Wound

Timid and afraid of relationships
Second guessing and judging motives
Extra cautious
Shut down sexually.
Shut down emotionally to happy feelings.

Crying often.
Unhealthy rumination of the past.
Pause and take care of yourself.

If the relationship was toxic, if there were more bad days than good days, if you are tired of settling for crumbs, acknowledge the behavioral patterns after a break-up. This way you will know what is around the curve and you will know how to establish your guardrails to protect yourself. Determine if you are numb emotionally and do foolish things just so you can feel something again, good, or bad.

When Addictive Relationship is over:
1. Abandonment wound.
2. Sadness with depression.
3. Continual confusion.
4. Powerless to say "no" if the person returns.
5. Repetitive mourning.
6. Rumination with offense.
7. Romanticizing the good and canceling the bad.
8. Euphoric recall may suck you out of reality back into toxic fairytale thinking. Then you recklessly drive around this mountain again.

You must recognize these relationship wounds so you can stop the addictive relationship thinking and protect yourself accordingly. Continue to study and educate yourself on how to heal yourself and break trauma bonds that lead to relationship addictions.

Work on identifying your relationship addiction behaviors. You know you are addicted to another if you can't stop thinking about them. You know you are prone to relationship addiction if you continually romanticize an invisible non-existent relationship or are obsessing in intense lust for a new person, you just met. If you are always looking for your other half as if part of you is missing, you are a sitting duck for toxicity. Soon we will develop our own identity and review the development of our safe inner self (Appendix C)

If we ever hope to have a peaceful home, we must change our patterns of communication. It is vital to separate physically when emotions are heated and return later with the ownership of our part of the problem. If both parties will return in an attitude of gentleness and forgiveness, the issues can be resolved quickly and peacefully. Then the communication can shift to gratefulness for the good the other person has done. Trust bonds can be established, and healthy relationships can grow. These communication skills take two willing people determined to learn the skills to love themselves and another.

Open Communication Skills
• Listening
• Problem solving
• Owning my part of the problem

• Gentleness
• Gratefulness
• Teachable attitude
• Compromise

Principle

Healing toxic thinking and relationship patterns makes space to develop healthy relationship skills.

Conclusion

Forgive Yourself

Childhood trauma was not your fault. But you can learn to grow and heal yourself. You can recognize toxic patterns and break bad habits and practice healthy communication skills.

Now you can rest, sing, and dance. Grace means there is no angry God. He is pursuing you with forgiveness. Now forgive yourself. Give yourself grace and mercy with a bucket full of tender loving-kindness.

Let your heart open and let yourself love again. Healing comes when you develop a safe self and a compassionate connection with yourself. Then will be able to connect with others whom you can safely love.

Father, it feels strange to think you would pursue me or that you would even care. It feels impossible to think a heavenly father isn't a condemning, angry judge waiting to cast me down. I hide myself from you. I fear I will never measure up and never be wanted.

Heal my heart from the inside. Let me see you as the loving father who cares, who provides, who protects, who desires to give me a good future. May I come to know you as a loving father who is compassionate, forgiving, gentle, gracious, and full of tender loving kindness. Amen.

LESSON 17

STAY/GO

If I agree with lies, I empower the liar.

Introduction

Addictive thinking

As I am sitting with the Lord this morning, I hear him reminding me that anger, fear, sorrow, or lust … strong impulsive repetitive thinking or behaviors are addictive. There are addictive chemicals leached in the brain that once formed develops ruts and dysfunctional unhealthy thinking patterns. These patterns are automatic. The negative thoughts come if my thinking is passive. Every possible quiet moment is flooded with noise. Even when there are no words, there is only anxiety. It takes as much recovery work to stop and change the toxic thinking patterns as it does to find chemical sobriety from substance use disorder.

Lesson

Thoughts may not be immediately destructive but will be traps in our lives to keep us entangled in toxicity. Contaminated thoughts cause recklessness, whining, obsessing, and an inability to see the truth. Embracing the stench of sick love keeps us totally stuck.

Sick vs Healthy love	
Sick	**Healthy**
Full of lust	Trusting
Suspicious	Caring
Controlling	Respectful
Dominate	Delightful
Paranoid	Comforting
Jealous	Enjoyment
Accusing	Excitement
Destructive	Fulfilling

If your relationship is both sick and healthy, if it vacillates between the two spectrums but has enough enjoyable days, stay. But set up boundaries to protect your peace and let the other person own their emotionally toxic and sick days. Correct your sick thoughts and exchange them for healthy ones. We an anchor. Let their emotions come and go but have no effect on you. This will take maturity.

Some of our loved ones have their own struggles and are unpleasable and moody. If we can let them have their space to have their own mood and not make it ours, we can still enjoy our day. The Rock of Recovery Detachment book teaches 12 principles to detaching from suffering.

If you can maintain your sanity and detach from the suffering and there are enough good days, then stay. If you are stuck, intensely suffering and regressing emotionally, leave or at least get temporary distance. It can be a week-by-week decision. Decisions don't have to be permanent, any movement or exercising your right to choose your destiny is powerful.

It takes maturity and practice to change thought patterns. <u>Changed thoughts patterns will lead to changed behavioral patterns.</u> If we can learn these skills, we can own our own space and develop a strong internal fortress to deflect the codependent injury of suffering for another.

A *codependent injury* is where we make ourselves responsible for someone else's happiness. Instead, we must return that responsibility to them.

Dead Marriage

Are you resistant to divorce from an emotionally/physically abusive partner?

Why have you resisted leaving? Outline your reasons to not leave?

Outline your reasons to leave?

Sometimes, we need to learn to pray. Journaling moves the toxicity outside of ourselves so it isn't repressed, and we can see it for what it is. Prayer releases the things we are powerless over to God.

Stay

Lord, I wait on you, please, give me a pure word. I want nothing for my life that you don't want for me. I will sacrifice and stay and recommit my prayers and my heart to invest in this failing marriage and divided family. I will do everything in my power to put it back together again and spare myself the heartache of divorce.

Make my path plain before me. Give me a decision-soaked in peace that I may know my next step.

Divorce

Lord, I will move on. Divorce. Bite the rag, endure the pain, wait for the sting of the curse to pass if that's what is best for me. Give me a word based upon your perfect will for my future. Not based upon my wounds, bitterness, sadness, rejection, abandonment, neglect, or confusion. Making a move in total confusion is a struggle. But if I knew next year would look like last year would this decision be so confusing? Lord, strengthen my heart. I will distance myself emotionally like I have left and learn to protect my own self until my path becomes plain.

Now write out three possible decisions you could make in this relationship. **Development of a safe internal self with detachment from suffering. This is self-preservation.**

Decision #1

Decision #2

Decision #3

Perpetual Grieving

A *chronic grieving cycle* is unhealthy perpetual sorrow. You can never seem to let go, resolve it, or move on. A chronic grieving cycle places you in the position of daily martyrdom.

Lord, why would I stay in a sick relationship? I am so love starved that I can't let go of the imaginary promises of future happiness. Surely, I have the skills to stop this and yet I can't get free. My journaling says this perpetual grieving that I am doing is idolatry. It feels like a toxic strain of emptiness and rejection that has me on a rumination replay of chronic bitterness. How could a decision be so elusive? How could it be so near and yet so far?

Write out the things that are causing you to grieve?

What would you lose if you left?

What would you gain if you left?

What would be the best thing for me?

What would a peaceful life look like?

What would I need to do to develop my half of a strong relationship? Is this even possible with this person?

What steps do I need to do to focus on my recovery?

What behaviors do I need to change?

Where do I need to heal?

What negative thoughts do I have every day that keep me stuck?

What healthy thoughts could I meditate on?

Lord, would you give me the strength to do the right thing? Would you help me? I am stuck! Everything within me is discouraged but wants to hope. Hope for what? That this marriage will magically heal itself? How dumb is that? How many years should I wait?

The fixer, empathic pleaser in me is toxic and I have lost myself. That is where I will start. I will start learning about my strengths and weaknesses.

What are my strengths?

What are my weaknesses?

Toxic Relationship Evaluation

I know a relationship is toxic if:

- I wake up at night rationalizing with an irrational person in my mind.
- We repeatedly have the same argument.
- All the problems at the beginning of this relationship are still present after years.
- I am intensely anxious when I think about being around this person.
- I am making myself very small and am trying to be invisible and walk on eggshells.

- I am compelled to keep going back and think there will be a different outcome.
- I keep repeating the same type of relationships.

Walk in your recovery one day at a time. Understand relationship addicts make excuses and are incapable of a healthy relationship without significant work. **It takes two whole people to make one healthy relationship.** This may take some time apart to accomplish. Relationship codependency leads to relationship addictions and are the center of the problem that empowers relapse and other addiction cycles. If you escape this toxic relationship, the next one is just around the corner. Do your own healing work.

Speak truth in love. Develop your own identity. Learn to trust yourself. Make others earn your trust. This needs to be at least a two-year journey. Do not tolerate any anger, or manipulation towards you or from you towards others or from your own internal critic.

> *Step back and have courage and trust that you can find your own path in life*

If you could make any decision, what would give you the most peace?

Application

In a toxic relationship, things may never really change. The love bombing may return for a moment, but soon the same argument reoccurs. The sick cycle of blaming and flipping your words and arguing returns. If your marriage/significant relationship has this kind of dynamic you probably spend all your energy, time and thoughts consumed with confusion. You may even mirror sick behaviors back at this person.

If you are passive, you lose yourself. If you fight back, things escalate. If you compromise, they push and bully you to position you under their control. You may give away your power to gain power in another area.

If you are told you are crazy for years and someone bashes you verbally on a regular basis, distance is necessary to even hear your own thoughts. If you know your thoughts and then they change when you are with this person, you are controlled, distance is needed. If you are depressed, distance is needed. If you are suicidal, distance is mandatory!

Depression and suicidal ideations in a toxic relationship are common. These are huge signals that you must find the strength to leave. You may have to leave ten times to be strong enough to totally remain free, but your life depends upon getting free.

I want you to take every repetitive stuck thought you have and flip it upside down.

- I can't leave.... I may not be able to leave today, but I can envision what that would look like tomorrow and plan.
- I can't make it on my own...I may have to live with a leaky air mattress for a bed and a lawn chair in the corner of an attic, but I can make it.
- They will kill me if I leave...I can go to a crisis shelter where they know how to protect me and establish legal means to procure more protection.

Now listen to the toxic lies one more time and change them. If we believe a lie, we empower the liar. It is time to take back my power. Flip your thoughts in this space below.

Domestic violence or any form of severe physical or verbal abuse is 100% **"exit now"** sign. Do what you must do to escape. Domestic violence shelter, homeless shelter, family member's basement... Do it now! You and your children are worth it. Get legal counsel. Empower yourself with lots of emotional support around you and listen to their counsel. No contact is best if possible. Use restraining orders and all legal means available to you to establish boundaries. The goal is freedom from abuse. This is a mental prison and your thoughts have been captured and are not your own. Listen to the words of others who work with those in domestic violence. You cannot trust yourself right now.

Principle

If I agree with lies, I empower the liar.

Conclusion

Shift and spend your energy secretly empowering yourself to acquire your freedom: mentally, financially, physically, and spiritually. Then, even if you decide to stay, you have developed trust in yourself and your ability to radically accept your loved one. They most likely won't change. But you won't be trying to manage someone else's happiness; you will return that job to them.

Now you can find you. It is your trust within yourself to do what is best for you and your children or those under your care that needs to be priority. Go to support groups, codependency groups, and counseling if that is available to you. If not, journal your inner thoughts. This will allow you to hear your fears and help you release your stressors. The problems will be out on paper. If problems are not pulled up out of your subconscious into your conscious thought processes, it will be impossible to stop the confusion and decide. The confusion will claim your future.

Lord, teach me to pray. Teach me to hear your voice clearly within my own heart. Help me to detach from the confusion and find a place of safety within myself. Give me the resolve to protect me and my children and to do the work necessary so I don't repeat this same scenario again. Set all the right people in my path to help me. Give me wise counsel and help me to have the courage to follow it. Amen.

LESSON 18

MARRIAGE

It takes two whole healthy people to make one lasting happy marriage.

Introduction

Finding Healthy Love

Healthy individuals will be able to **securely attach**. They won't be too quick to connect but steady and allow the relationship to grow. There will allows be a **respect of boundaries**. You will never feel pressured or bullied. Their communication skills will be **kind and gentle**. They will be **quick to resolve** any disagreements. They will **respect you** and speak to you and others with **manners.** There will be a mutual attraction and compatible energy with **future**

goals. They have had years or even decades of **stability** and can securely connect. **They will mean what they say** and not be internally conflicted. These are your goals forward to finding a healthy, stable relationship.

Lesson

Internal conflict will be exhibited with insecure behaviors. This will make any relationship unstable and prevent a healthy attachment. Study insecure attachment styles. Broken people will not be able to attach in a healthy manner. You will observe behaviors of dominance with control, avoidance with the inability to be present, push-pull behaviors, I want you, oh no, I don't want you, people-pleasing that is overly servant-like, excessive gift giving or constantly apologizing, and victim behaviors such as self-pity, whining, intense anxiety, and/or frequent mood swings.

Exercise

Work through these relationship evaluations.

Mr. or Mrs. Possible Evaluation	
1) Their words must match their walk.	
2) They must be willing to do the work to be emotionally available.	
3) They must be emotionally mature and able to rise above their emotions and do what is right.	

4) They must spend the time to earn your trust.	
5) They must come after you but not be overly jealous.	
6) Its nice when they watch and study you and know what you like and don't like. This attentiveness will develop relationship growth.	
7) Consistency is key; and a teachable attitude is a necessity.	
8) Emotional stability is a strong indicator that the other person is available for a relationship. *Mood swings are a hot red flag. *Frequent exaggerated emotions are a stop sign.	

When it is right:	
1) Your heart is full of love for this person. You will feel safe and relaxed and calm. Nothing will need to be forced.	
2) You can't wait to be with them.	
3) You want to share everything with them.	
4) They have the capacity to give and receive love.	
5) They hear and see you and can speak your love language.	
6) They are not entangled in past relationships.	
7) They can securely attach to you.	
8) You can share anything and be your **true authentic self**.	

Is Marriage Right for You?	
1) Will marriage bring you stability, safety, and security?	

2) Will marriage strip you of your money and power? Do they have their own financial stability, or do they want you to finance their dream?	
3) Do their words and actions match?	
4) What is their relationship like with their parents, children, and x-spouses? Do they handle broken relationships with kindness or bitterness?	
5) Do they respect people in authority over them?	
6) Do they have a good work ethic?	
7) Do they have good character?	
8) Are they kind?	
9) Do you trust them?	

Motives are tricky. *Reckless intimacy* with a one-night stand can be exciting feelings of affection and attention. Healthy individuals run away and see a quick hook-up as toxic. Unhealthy people rush in head long following their passions and think they will have a different outcome than their last reckless endeavor.

When the caution signs go on, is it too late? Are you already involved sexually which will cloud your judgment? Quick movement in new relationships is the hallmark sign of past trauma. They medicate themselves with the quick sex I call *reckless intimacy*. This regulates their ego and gives them a quick fix. Both people are burned. Work through these self-evaluation questions in your journal.

Motives and other things to consider	
1) Are you ever afraid to say no?	
2) Do you think this is a one-time opportunity?	
3) Can you hold a part of yourself back and get to know someone slowly?	
4) Do you have the skills to discern reality of who this person really is and move out quickly?	
5) Do you look at who this person really is or who they could be?	
6) Can you take the time to see through a fake persona?	
7) Can you share deep conversations without physical contact?	
8) What might a future with this person look like?	
9) Is this person a suitable life partner?	
10) Do you have common interest?	
11) Are you compatible?	
12) Is there adequate means to provide for a home together?	
13) Are you moving in together too quickly for convenience's sake?	
14) Are there children involved that will need a stepparent?	
15) Are their nasty X spouses to deal with?	

Application

How broke are you?

If you are broken, you are vulnerable. If you are love starved, you're a sitting duck and will be devoured. You're an easy target.
If you need: attention, affirmation, validation, approval, physical touch, words of affection, being known and seen and loved and on and on… you are going to be helpless in a new relationship and will lose yourself quickly. Have a healthy sanctified love for yourself. Don't be a victim of your past. Find your confidence and heal yourself first.

Relationship Evaluation	
1) Is the relationship distracting you from your life calling?	
2) Is it supportive of your future goals?	
3) Can you see reality? Does the words and actions match?	
4) Does it feel like an emotional roller coaster?	
5) Does the person want a deep connection that is long term or just excitement of a new partner?	
6) Is there a heart ache with this person's conflicting behaviors? Do they want you and another person at the same time?	
7) What is this relationship costing you?	
8) Does this relationship bring out a playful, immature side of you that feels irresponsible?	

9) Are they capable of giving you the intimacy, validation, and affection you need?	
10) Did the relationship start well and once they got you hooked, and now you are settling for scraps?	
11) Is this person capable of being an equal partner?	
12) Is this person teachable, growing and maturing or regressing emotionally?	

Stay back a safe distance physically until the emotions are sorted out. It takes a couple weeks to a couple months for both partners to decide if this feels right to them. If you have delayed sexual intimacy, you can think clearly.

It may always feel right at the beginning. It is only when the heat of passion slows to a simmer that you can analyze the depth of this person's character and emotional availability. Decide if you are just lusting after this person or if you are talking yourself into being with them. Value yourself enough to keep a safe distance and watch out for yourself.

Six months...No impulsivity

If it is true love, then it will be clear in 6 months. Wait 6 months, and you will either be thrilled you dodged a crazy person, or you will have built a foundation of trust that could develop into a satisfying and fulfilling relationship. No impulsivity.

Years ago, I believed every word a new person said to me. I believed the image they projected of themselves. My empathy was too strong, and I would attract abusive bullies pretending to be victims who were looking for a rescuer.

Now I keep quiet and think, I wonder how much of this is for my entertainment. If their speech sounds rehearsed, they may be so convincing because they now believe their own lies. Get your discerning wires tuned to identify half-truths, fake personalities and outright lies. You will be incapable of doing this if you are so needy you are gullible or already sexual involved.

List the attributes of the life partner you desire?

What attitudes, actions or character flaws will you not tolerate?

Self-Regulation

When I feel profound anxiety that dysregulates me and makes me feel out of control, I need to self-sooth or learn self-regulation. These may be adolescent skills I did not learn. First, let's identify the feeling of my heart that is causing this dysregulation.

1) What is my feeling? Do I feel lonely, unloved, rejected, neglected, or angry? Am I trying to control a person or an outcome?

2) Can I identify my imbalance? Am I stuck in my head obsessing? Am I stuck in an emotion I can't process? How often do I do this? How much does it take to trigger me into anxiety?

3) Do I indulge negative emotions? Do I ruminate and obsess until I torment myself and then engage dysfunctional coping skills?

4) Have I given myself space to heal? Do I slow down and process my anxiety when I feel it? Do I take time every morning to make sure I am calm when I start my day and every evening to discharge the toxicity of the day and release it?

5) Am I empathy queen? Do I take on the problems of other people? How easily can I walk away and let someone else suffer for their own choices?

6) Can I choose a free spirit and detach from anxious thoughts and circumstances and enjoy my day? Do I numb myself with television or other activities?

7) Can I choose to not enable another person to make excuses for their poor behavior or their poor choices? Can I let another person have their own emotion and not let it affect me?

8) Can I acknowledge anxiety and process its origin? Is this a repetitive pattern of waiting for the next crisis even when nothing bad is happening now? If so, this is a trauma response that needs healed.

9) Choking anxiety needs intervention. It needs the body to learn to regulate with self-soothing. There are many programs on how to heal trauma and how to take control of your breath and your thoughts. This may be something you want to explore. If you rate your anxiety level ten times today, what would it be? How much peace can you hold onto?

Principle

It takes two whole healthy people to make one lasting happy marriage.

Conclusion

True Lover

Allowing another person, the freedom to come, stay or go and to choose what is best for them without any pressure makes for a *secure attachment*. Emotional maturity does not entangle new relationships with past rejection, abandonment, and neglect issues.

Having a true lover is only possible if you are a whole person and don't need someone else to complete you. The relationship can only be healthy when there are no expectations but radical acceptance of personal differences. Then you both can allow the other person to remain an individual and adopt a supportive role to the other.

When two people are emotionally healthy and safe within their own identity, then you can stay in the present and enjoy every stinking moment with delight to please and nurture each other.

Here's what it looks like to be whole:

Self-actualization
1. Peaceful and calm
2. Joyful
3. Authentic
4. Self-regulate
5. Empathy
6. Kindness
7. Compassion
8. Emotional Stability

Lord, continue to help me value myself and to understand my self-worth. Give me courage to heal from old trauma wounds and to rewrite my future to look different than my past. Help me to be faithful to not betray myself. Give me great contentment and joy with my own life so that I will not be seeking outside of our relationship for fulfillment. Help me to wait on you to bring me the significant other you have for me. Amen.

LESSON 19

IDENTITY

A lack of identity and self-worth creates internal chaos which will be acted out externally in relationships.

Introduction

Fake Self

A child that was not accepted and allowed to develop a strong identity will conform to who they think others want them to be. This will lead to a fake self.

True intimacy is developed when there is an ability to be connected and accepted for your real self. A relationship with a kind and safe person will (over time) develop a bond of security and help us heal enough that we can develop our true authentic self.

Lesson

Building an Identity

Often an adult with a traumatic childhood did not develop their own identity. Instead, they conformed to whatever they think the parent or teacher expects. They may develop a *fake-identity* and become a performer or a perfectionist.

Then they are like a child and thrive from praise for their performance. And/or they always beat themselves up because they aren't perfect. Self-focus becomes dominant, and everything is about their inner pain.

Others had such a loud complaining parent that they develop a strong internal critic that speaks of self-condemnation and hatred for themselves to the point that they give up on living a successful life.

Then they may identify with self-destructive forces through drug addiction, alcoholism, or criminal activities. This acts out the unsafe environment externally that developed internally within this person.

This is problematic in recovery. Without a strong identity of who you are internally, there will be a development of unhealthy sick attachments. This is apparent when sex becomes the norm in the first few hours after meeting someone new. Or when there is intense dominance and control early on in a relationship. Or when your fears overrun you and you lash out at others.

Without a safe environment, anger can be a learned skill of survival to protect yourself. Whatever age you were when you were traumatized is what age you feel like when you drop into an emotionally regressed state. This regressed state will trigger a fight, flight, freeze or fawn response. It will not be emotionally mature and able to navigate daily life struggles. Hence, the importance of developing a safe inner self with a strong identity of who you are and what you will and will not do is vital for your stability.

Exercise

Identify characteristics of a strong identity and where you have room to grow.

BUILDING MY OWN IDENTITY

Building my own identity gives me confidence to trust my decisions.	
1. Do I permit myself to have a day of rest every week?	
2. Can I allow myself to have one frivolous unproductive hour a day?	
3. Can I recognize what disturbs my inner peace and refuse it?	

4. Can I instruct myself to wait patiently and refuse to fret?	
5. Can I be slow to make decisions? Can I be slow to be angry? Can I listen to others?	
6. Can I refuse impulsive decisions and make a well thought out plan of action?	
7. Can I be quiet inside and confident that all will be well…no matter what?	
8. Can I recognize that some people will never have inner peace and that it's, ok?	
9.Can I recognize when I have an imbalance and then get alone to rebalance myself?	
10. Can I accept my weaknesses?	
11. Can I be kind to myself?	
12. Can I keep my heart open and not judge others?	
13. Can I protect my heart with a firm boundary without shutting others out?	
14. Can I choose each moment what I will and will not think?	
15. If I stray into a negative thinking trap, how quickly can I recover myself?	
16. Can I trust myself to release bitterness and forgive often?	
17. Can I find or hope to find another safe person with whom to share life?	
18. Can I enjoy being alone?	
19. Can I reject manipulative, abusive people without any guilt?	

20. Can I have confidence in my abilities to make right choices?	
21. Can I address my inner double-talk that brings confusion and stand still until I know what to do?	
22. Can I let go of my regrets?	
23. Can I stop my fretting?	
24. Am I free to say no to others? Do I know my limits?	
25. Can I stop forcing my way onto others?	
26. Can I focus on the good and let go of the bad?	
28. Can I reshape the bad and find good in everything?	
29. Can I not sweat the small stuff?	
30. Do I take care of myself physically, emotionally, mentally, financially, and spiritually?	

Without our own identity, we may continue to gravitate to relationships that are steeped in domestic violence or active addiction. If we don't have a healthy identity, we are attracted to unhealthy people. Then we are enmeshed in another person's personality as our source and are hyper focused on pleasing or controlling them and lose whatever recovery we may have recently established.

The key to recovery from depression, anxiety, trauma, domestic violence, or any kind of addiction is to build our own identity, your own self-worth.

Application

Evaluate your unworthy feelings and work a recovery plan to understand you are precious. *...so may my life be precious this day in the sight of the Lord, and may he deliver me out of all tribulation. 1 Samuel 26:24*

Unworthy	
1) Feeling not worthy	
2) Needing to martyr myself and maybe my tears will move God.	
3) Manipulating others with tears, self-pity, sorrow, etc.	
4) Codependent control freak	
5) Forcing my will and not releasing my will to God.	
6) Self-abuse through a negative internal critic	
7) Refusing to be comforted	
8) Poverty spirit with a slave attitude	
9) Religious spirit with lots of rules.	
10) Feeling like I never fit in.	

Cure	
1) Recognize what comes from heaven and what comes from hell.	
2) Practice detaching from everything that causes you suffering.	
3) Let go and trust God	

4) Embrace the joy and peace of the kingdom of God	
5) Practice emotional maturity	
6) Recognize comfort and allow others to comfort you.	
7) Now go and comfort others.	
8) Get a vision for a different future.	
9) Take small steps to build your independence and confidence	
10) Do what is right for your safety and sanity and then become emotionally detached and indifferent to outcomes.	
11) Move any intense negative emotion outside of yourself and observe it and let it become your teacher, but not your identity.	
12) Work on self-control so you can learn to trust yourself.	

Visualization skill

If you feel unworthy, you are holding garbage. Dump hands full of garbage and release it again and again until you are allowed to fill your hands with goodness. You cannot hold good and bad at the same time. Develop a vision for the kingdom of heaven. Refuse the nonsense and receive the good.

Principle

A lack of identity and self-worth creates internal chaos which will be acted out externally in relationships.

Conclusion

If you pick a relationship where you start to lose yourself and start feeling like a victim or a pleaser who is walking on eggshells, back up quickly before you become trapped and lose your power to do so. If your new relationship feels confusing, take a break. You probably have learned to not trust your instincts.

Trust your intuition for a moment. If you are wrong, the boundary of a little space and time will strengthen a healthy relationship. If you excuse all the red flags, well, you're still sick and going to get hurt.

Sexual wounds will heal when you heal. You won't panic with the thought of being touched. Physical touch will be comforting and not make you want to recoil.

You won't be impulsive and hypersexualized. You won't rush relationships but allow them to build trust and grow naturally. You won't be attracting emotionally unavailable people with lots of instability when you have a strong identity within yourself.

You won't be trying to fix someone else. You won't choose brokenness. You won't need to fix another to make yourself feel whole. You won't be distracted easily.

You can be complete in yourself with or without a relationship. You can be sad when a relationship ends, but if the relationship isn't your identity, it will be easier to learn and grow from it and keep moving forward as mature adults can do. It won't be the end of the world and end in relapse or self-destructive behaviors.

Develop your own identity. Learn to love yourself in a healthy sanctified manner. Learn to enjoy your own company and allow yourself the ability to laugh again.

Lord, it is me. You know I am made of dirt. You know I can't do this by myself. I don't even know if I can trust myself to stay on course for one day. Give me solid ground beneath my feet and steady me. Empower me to set boundaries and trust myself to follow through and do the work to reclaim my life.

Empower me to set boundaries with others and to enforce them. Give me the courage to walk away if I need to do so for my future. Protect me as I grow. Protect me until I am big inside and can protect myself. Give me a strong "no" muscle and teach me how to use it. Amen.

LESSON 21

SEXUAL SOBRIETY

Casual sex clouds your judgment and attracts toxic relationships.

Introduction

Fear of the Lord is the key to recovery. Agreeance with the Word of God is my job. Rationalizing and excusing is dangerous. If God's Word is true, then it is not debatable. If I am hypersexualized, I have emotional wounds and lots of trust issues.

Likely I struggle to connect, and the physical act of sex makes me feel connected but if I don't move from sexual intimacy into emotional intimacy I will not likely grow and mature in any relationship. A mature person will start with emotional intimacy first and allow a trust bond to form and then move to physical intimacy.

I cannot make up my own rules regarding sex.
just because I live in a sex saturated culture.
Can I get away with it? Maybe.
Will I get hurt? Probably.
Will I hurt someone else? Definitely

Lesson

What if I just wrangled my flesh and practiced purity. Well, this thing is bigger than me. There is nothing in me that wants chastity. What if I just asked God for the grace to be virtuous? What if I ran like Joseph, the Hebrew slave, who chose prison over the advancements of his master's wife? What would it look like for me to not make any provision for my flesh to fulfill its lust?

I don't think you will ever be sorry that you chose the high ground. If the relationship is supposed to be, then it will still be in 6-12 months.

Know that if you are driven like a dog and cannot stop yourself, it isn't real. It won't last. It is just another addiction. Sex …the chase…the game… this will just feed the addictive patterns in your brain.

Casual sex without true commitment usually ends in disaster. Premarital sex may connect you emotionally to a partner that you never wanted in the first place and that isn't a good companion.

Early sex in a relationship clouds all your judgment.

Noxious Rationalizations
Lust is a beguiling serpent. It slithers and it lies, and it twists your thinking.
1. "Did God really say....?"
2. "Aren't we under grace now?"
3. "As long as no one gets hurt?"
4. "We are adults, we can choose?"

Exercise

Pray for a pure heart.

Biblical Instructions
So, flee youthful lusts: but follow righteousness, faith, charity, peace, with them that call on the Lord out of a pure heart. 2 Timothy 2:22 KJV
Do not be deceived: Neither the sexually immoral nor idolaters nor adulterers ...will inherit the kingdom of God. 1 Corinthians 6:9

> *For if you live according to the flesh, you will die; but if by the Spirit you put to death the misdeeds of the body, you will live. Romans 8:13*

You can make a choice, but you can't control the damage that will happen afterwards.

Navigating Purity

In today's sex crazed culture, it is very difficult to navigate purity to the standard of the generations in the past. It is a real blessing if you can. Like Paul said in *1 Corinthians 7:8 Now to the unmarried and the widows I say: It is good for them to stay unmarried, as I do. But if they cannot control themselves, they should marry...*

Paul, the apostle, says there is trouble in relationships. So, consider having less relationships to have less trouble. I would like to make marriage the standard for sexual intimacy, but since relationships start so quickly you really have no clue who you would be marrying. For those who have been raised in church all their lives or desire to keep their virginity until marriage, you are taking the high road and will surely be blessed.

But for those who were molested as young children or started having sex as pre-teens, let me raise the bar from one-night stands, casual sex, fairytale mentality of instant romance, and develop a healthy respect for yourself a year or more without a relationship to give yourself time to heal.

Holiness

Holiness, purity, sexual sobriety is a gift from God, no one can find it without humility and grace.

Repentance

When I repent in the flesh, I beat myself up, condemn myself, do penance, and have no power to stop sinning. The shame makes me hide from the Lord.

The feelings of low self-esteem can trigger old abandonment wounds, separation anxiety and chronic grieving. This can trigger chronic grieving and release an avalanche of lifetime losses that need grieved and released.

Once I recognize the trauma wounds of separation anxiety and the chronic grieving, I can pull it up out of my subconscious and feel it until I can find a piece of gratitude and see things differently. Take the grief of loss and disappointment and turn it upside down and see it in a hundred ways: good and bad. What did you learn? How did you grow? How can you help others? Gratitude for my life experiences can bring me to acceptance. Acceptance is a place of peace.

Now, learn to release intense passion when it comes. If it belongs to you, it will return. If not, let it move on and reclaim yourself.

Application

Develop a sexually sobriety plan that will work for you.

Sexual Sobriety Plan
1) You must want to be Sexually Sober.
2) You must pray and decide what is acceptable and what is toxic in your life.
3) Repent and ask God for help. Set boundaries.
4) Repent repeatedly and ask for deliverance until you find the strength to say no.
5) Practice saying no to yourself in other areas, money, food, chocolate, sleep, tv, games, etc.
6) Set up disciplines in your life.
7) Make Christ your first love.
8)Build a relationship with God and wait on his timing.
9)Get an accountability partner.
10)Remember no imaginary fantasy. Turn on your conscience and correct your limerent/fairytale thinking.

For sound advice is a beacon, good teaching is a light, moral discipline is a life path. They'll protect you from promiscuous women, from the seductive talk of some temptress. Don't lustfully fantasize on her beauty, nor be taken in by her bedroom eyes.

You can buy an hour with a prostitute for a loaf of bread, but a promiscuous woman may well eat you alive. Can you build a fire in your lap and not burn your pants? Can you walk barefoot on hot coals and not get blisters?

Its' the same when you have sex with your neighbor's wife: Touch her and you'll pay for it. No excuses. Hunger is no excuse for a thief to steal... Adultery is a brainless act, soul-destroying, self-destructive...Proverbs 6:24-32 MSG

No amount of shame, guilt or self-condemnation can change the past only the blood of Jesus can sanctify and redeem what I have lost.

Principle

Casual sex clouds your judgment and attracts toxic relationships.

Conclusion

One day Sober

Rehearse your goals: Protect your future. Start thinking of yourself as cherished and precious. Protect your sanity by thinking healthy thoughts. Learn to become safe for yourself. Forgive, heal, and bless others. Make it your life goal to not hurt or use anyone. When you heal, you won't be so love starved and impulsive and will be free to make better decisions for yourself and your family. Now work a sexual sobriety plan and walk it out along with your recovery from substance use disorder and all its associated traumas.

Help me, Lord. Help me not to stumble. Help me to see a token of my identity and calling so I can raise the bar higher. Teach me to fellowship with you and feel like I have a loving father to protect me. Let my heart burn with love for you and others. Now may you take everything meant for evil and turn it to good. Give me a spiritual awakening this day that I may believe, Amen.

LESSON 22

JESUS FRIEND OF SINNER

Jesus loves the Broken.

Introduction

The power of our relationships can make us whole or break us. A heart that burns with the love of Christ is strong enough to love ourselves and others. Our healing journey starts with the release of our emotional pain. **If we can nurture a friendship with Jesus, our traumas wounds will resolve.** The acceptance of the Savior who gave his life for us can take us to a place of self-love and inner fulfillment. The growth we can experience is exponential.

Lesson

Jesus loves sinners. He hung out and ate with sinners. (Matthew 9:10) He was comfortable to be with those who knew they were broken. (Mark 2:17) He didn't hang out with those who were fake and performed for outward approval. (Matthew 3:7) There are warnings for hypocrites about not praying publicly on the street corner to make a show. (Matthew 6:7) Jesus warns not to announce what you were giving. Not to let the left hand know what the right hand was doing. Matthew 6:3 says to go into your closet in secret and seek for your heavenly father. Matthew 6:6

There is a hidden inner chamber inside our heart when it is empty, we are seeking, searching, and grasping in the dark for something to fill it. But only the Savior can fill our heart and make it burn with a deep satisfaction. Things of this world can fill us temporarily but only the Master can make us whole again. Perhaps you are using temporal things to fill the void in your soul?

But many who are first will be last, and the last will be first. Mark 10:31 Jesus loves sinners. He knows our helpless condition and has compassion for us. *For God so loved the world that he gave his one and only Son, that whoever believes in him shall not perish but have eternal life. John 3:16*

Mary Magdalene was the first to see Jesus after resurrection. Mary was a woman that was delivered from seven demons. Luke 8:2 And yet, she was the one that he chose first to reveal himself to when he arose from the tomb. John 20:15 She had risen early to go and anoint him at the grave. She was crying for him. When he spoke her name, she recognized him as the risen Savior. Her heart cry was "Rabboni" which means teacher. She allowed Jesus to teach her his love. Mary had not recognized him through her tears until he spoke her name, Mary. Then her heart knew it was Jesus. Can you hear the Master speak your name?

Prostitute washing the feet of Jesus *Luke 7:39,44-50 NIV.*

When the Pharisee who had invited him saw this, he said to himself, "If this man were a prophet, he would know who is touching him and what kind of woman she is-that she is a sinner." [44] Then he (Jesus) turned toward the woman and said to Simon, "Do you see this woman? I came into your house. You did not give me any water for my feet, but she wet my feet with her tears and wiped them with her hair. [45] You did not give me a kiss, but this woman, from the time I entered, has not stopped kissing my feet. [46] You did not put oil on my head, but she has poured perfume on my feet. [47] Therefore, I tell you, her many sins have been forgiven-as her great love has shown. But whoever has been forgiven little loves little." [48] Then Jesus said to her, "Your sins are forgiven." [49] The other guests began to say among themselves, "Who is this who even forgives sins?" [50] Jesus said to the woman, "Your faith has saved you; go in peace."

Woman at the Well A woman from Samaria came to draw water and Jesus asked her for a drink. Jews weren't allowed to speak to Samaritans. She questioned him on why he was asking for a drink from her since the religious rules forbid him to speak to her. John 4:7-30 Jesus says to her, *everyone who drinks this water will be thirsty again, but whoever drinks the water I give them will never thirst. Indeed, the water I give them will become in them a spring of water welling up to eternal life."*

Then Jesus tells her to go call her husband and she says I have no husband. He speaks to her kindly and tells her, *"You are right when you say you have no husband. The fact is, you have had five husbands, and the man you now have is not your husband. What you have just said is quite true."*

Jesus breaks religious rules to speak to a despised Samaritan and a woman, he does not judge or condemn her. He tells her he is the way to eternal life and reveals to her that he is the Messiah.

Woman Caught in Adultery John 8:1-11 The pharisees brought Jesus a woman that was caught in adultery. The law said she had to be stoned. They were trying to trap Jesus and make him condemn her. Instead, he bent down and started to write on the ground with his finger and he said to them, *"Let anyone who is without sin be the first to throw a stone at her."* Then her accusers left, and he told her to *"go and sin no more."* This is grace. Give yourself grace and give grace to others.

Grandma's Of Jesus

Tamar Genesis 38 Her husband died. She had no children and Judah, her father-in-law, was supposed to give her to his next son. But he didn't. So, she played a prostitute and slept with Judah and God blessed her with twins. One of her sons Pharez, was in the line from Judah to King David to Jesus.

Rahab, the prostitute in Joshua Chapters 2 & 6, spared the spies and was spared when Jericho was destroyed. She was received as one of the Israelites and married Salmon and became a mother to Boaz and grandmother to King David from whom the lineage of Jesus came forth.

Ruth Book of Ruth a Moabite received a kinsman redeemer, named Boaz. She married Boaz and he became the father of Obed and Obed was the father of Jesse and Jesse was the father of King David and therein lies the heritage of Jesus. *Book of Ruth*

Bathsheba 2 Samuel 11 She was desired and taken by King David, and her husband, Uriah, was then essentially murdered by David. David ordered his General, Joab, to place Uriah on the front line of the battle and withdraw support from him and this would mean certain death for Uriah. David and Bathsheba's first child died. Bathsheba's second son, Solomon, became king of Israel and from this line came Jesus.

These women were a demonstration of God's forgiveness. His love and grace can redeem your past and is an example of his forgiveness to all.

Exercise

Use one of these verses below and journal what Jesus would say to you.

Application

If Jesus loves the rejected, then he loves me.

Others Jesus loved:

Zacchaeus Luke 19 Jesus hung out with sinners and ate with despised tax collector. Zacchaeus welcomed Jesus to his house. He gave half his possessions to the poor and vowed to pay back four times the amount to anyone he had cheated. This man's heart was changed. Has your heart changed?

Tax Collector Matthew 9:9 Matthew was sitting at the tax collector's booth, and he heard the call "follow me" and became a disciple of Jesus. This man heard the call to follow Jesus. No matter where you are at in life, can you hear the call on your life?

Man in the temple, a pharisee and a tax collector. The pharisee went to the temple and worshipped himself. The tax collector beat his breast and said, "God, have mercy on me, a sinner." He unable to look up from shame. Luke 18:10-14 Which man walked away justified?

Broken and Contrite heart Ps 34:18 The Lord is close to the brokenhearted and saves those who are crushed in spirit. Psalm 51:17

God never despises a broken and contrite heart. How broken is your heart?

<u>Lost</u> Psalm 119:176 The psalmist says he is lost and ask the Lord to come and seek for him. Matthew 18:11 The shepherd leaves the 99 safe sheep and goes and looks for the one that is lost. If you feel lost, have you asked the Savior to come and find you?

<u>Thief on the cross</u> Luke 23:39-43 Jesus was hung on the cross between two criminals. The one criminal mocked him and the other asked Jesus to remember him. *Jesus said, "Truly I tell you, today you will be with me in paradise."*

Broken

Lord, help me. I am broken. Help us to work recovery in all areas of our life. Help us to take dominion over every thought and line it up with the Word of God.

Can a wounded heart and rejection drive me so deep into nonsense that I lose sight of you, my Lord? Obviously so! How can I find my way back? There must be a way back because of the work you did for me on the cross.

Is it true? Are you really a God of love and mercy? My heart is so broken that I can't imagine anyone ever really loving me. I feel all the suffering and betrayals stole my love affair with you, my Lord. Preserve me through the times of darkness. I so doubt myself that I find it difficult to pray and difficult to read the Word and difficult to settle in and find my peace. The racing thoughts are overwhelming. Send your Word and deliver me, my Lord. Amen Psalm 107:20

Grounded in the Word

Ground me in your Word. Ground me in my calling and give me a vision for the future. Help me stop the distractions and stop the confusion by just moving forward. Amen. Ephesians 3:17

Goodness of God

Is it true, Lord? Are you good? Is your goodness going to chase me down? Will you give me the power to stop and return to you with my whole heart? Will you give me your favor, Lord? Deuteronomy 28:2

The Gift of Repentance

Lord, help me position myself beneath your loving arms with a heart full of peace. Help me to stop my foolish thinking and take high ground above the attacks. I am truly helpless without your embrace. Help me find a place to receive the gift of repentance. Amen. Psalm 18:33; 57:1; Matthew 3:8

Principle

God loves the broken.

Conclusion

Jesus didn't come for the righteous (self-righteous). He came for those who knew they needed a physician. Those who knew they were sick. (Mark 2:17) Jesus didn't call the leaders or teachers of the law, he called laborers (fisherman). He used the simple to confound the wise. 1 Corinthians 3:18-19

The first-person Jesus reveals himself to after his resurrection was Mary Magdalene, a woman who had been delivered from seven demons. The first time Jesus reveals himself as the Messiah is to an immoral, despised Samaritan woman at the well. There were four questionable women in his ancestry line.

Jesus seems to prefer the broken and likes the underdogs. He came to seek and save those who were lost. He loves the rejected. He made the last first and the first last. His harshest words of criticism were for the arrogant and proud leaders *"You brood of vipers! Who warned you to flee from the wrath to come? Matthew 3:7*

Oh Lord, God of Mercy, if you are the God of mercy… your grace covers all. See my wounded heart, Lord, and send me your comforter. Let your forgiveness run so deep that I would never think about my past or what I have done, but only your peace and a trusting relationship with you. Let the fervor of my heart be connection to you. May your love bind me in such a way that no one could pry me loose from your hand and no one could speak a false word that I could not discern. Amen.

APPENDIX A: HIGHER AND LOWER LEVELS OF LOVE

Beloved means: one who is greatly loved.

DEVELOPMENTAL STAGES OF LOVE

Lower levels of love

1. **Self-love** – empty, lonely, using others. Characterized by a life of confusion.

People will be lovers of themselves, lovers of money, boastful, proud, abusive, disobedient to their parents, ungrateful, unholy, without love, unforgiving, slanderous, without self-control, brutal, not lovers of the good, treacherous, rash, conceited, lovers of pleasures rather than lovers of God – having a form of godliness but denying its power. Have nothing to do with them. 2 Timothy 3:2-5

2. **False Love** – kind speech in mouth, but not in heart. This type of love is very irritating.

If I speak in the tongues of men and of angels, but have not love, I am only a resounding gong or a clanging cymbal. 1 Corinthians 13:1

3. **Enabling Love** – This person understands consequences and tries to remove the mountains in other people's lives.

Most usually these mountains are particularly important so that the person can grow and mature and become strong. This person has faith, but their faith is usually in themselves or in their money.

If I have a gift of prophecy and can fathom all mysteries and all knowledge, and If I have a faith that can move mountains, but have not love, I am nothing. 1 Corinthians 13:2

4. **Best Effort Love** – This person does a lot of charity work and gives of themselves. They do this to look good or to make up for other things in their lives that are not right. This type of love can be motivated by guilt or a need for approval and acceptance.

If I give all I possess to the poor and surrender my body to the flames, but have not love, I gain nothing. 1 Corinthians 13:3

Higher levels of love: Understanding my purpose in life

5. **True Love** – Patient and Kind. This person wrestles their own stubborn self-will and pins it to the ground and pursues being a person that loves this way. **This person repents often.**

Love is patient, love is kind. It does not envy, it does not boast, it is not proud. It is not rude, it is not self-seeking, it is not easily angered, it keeps no record of wrongs. Love does not delight in evil but rejoices with the truth. It always protects, always trusts, always hopes, always perseveres.

Love never fails. 1 Corinthians 13:4-8a

6. **Tough love** – This love is strong enough to allow others to have their own free will and make their own choices and suffer their own consequences. This person trust that others can find their own path.

I urge you, brothers, to watch out for those who cause divisions and put obstacles in your way that are contrary to the teaching you have learned. Keep away from them. Romans 16:17-19

7. **Perfect Love** – Characterized by having no fear. Speaks truth to himself frequently and wrestles fears and pins them to the ground.

There is no fear in love. But perfect love drives out fear because fear has to do with punishment (torment). 1 John 4:18

8. **Love your Higher Power and your neighbor as yourself**. This love is pure and seeks opportunity to help those in genuine need.

Jesus replied: "'Love the Lord your God with all your heart and with all your soul and with all your mind.' This is the first and greatest commandment. And the second is like it: 'Love your neighbor as yourself.' All the Law and the Prophets hang on these two commandments." Matthew 22:37-40

9. **Love with great peace** – This person will never take offense. But he will instead bear the burden of others. This person visits the sick and makes meals for those with cancer or with a new baby. This person keeps their schedule loose enough to plan for the little interruptions in life.

Great peace have they who love your law, and nothing can make them stumble (offended). Psalm 119:165; Carry each other's burdens, and in this way, you will fulfill the law of Christ. Galatians 6:2

10. **Everlasting love** – This love transcends time, space and all eternity and will love forever. This is a love that is more powerful than life. This is a place of safety and honor. When there is higher level of faithful, devoted, selfless reciprocal love and devotion, you can be greatly loved and find someone you can greatly love and be someone's beloved.

...I have loved you with an everlasting love; I have

drawn you with loving-kindness. Jeremiah 31:3

> *Finding mature love means letting go of the lower levels of love. This will allow you to give and receive higher levels of love.*

Think Effective Boundaries – At times, you may need to draw near your loved ones. At other times, you may need to move back from them to allow them space to work through the developmental stages of love.

Here are some behaviors to identify true love from false love:

LOVE IS...LOVE IS NEVER

Love is....	Love is never....
Peaceful	Demeaning
Gentle	Demanding
Kind	Abusive
Rewarding	Neglectful
Caring	Manipulative
Sharing	Hateful/Selfish
Patient	Argumentative
Forgiving	Vengeful
Always wanting best for others	Controlling; demanding own way
Working it out together	Fearful
Talking it out together	Full of should & should not
Respectful	Resentful/Bitter

Trusting	Accusatory
Forgetting the past	Never forgetting the past/shaming
Giving and helping	Selfish/self-centered
Always thinking of how to encourage others	Discouraging
Always uplifts another	Tearing down the esteem of another
Allows freedom to make their own choices	Yelling and angry
Allows person to receive consequences for poor choices.	Manipulates other people emotionally and bullies to get them to do what they want
Hopes for the best	Denies there is a problem
Refuses emotional manipulation	Accepts consequences or interrupts them (enabler)
Gets wise counsel, ponders each word spoken and each deed done.	Decisions based on emotions
Seeks help for self when stuck emotionally	Throws money at a problem to "fix it"
Sets standard and a plan	Makes excuses for themselves and others
Sticks to the plan/Accountable	Smooths things over
Willing to suffer for right decisions	Hides things
Willing to avoid rebellious people if needed	Everyone must get along at all costs
Always kind, but firm	Easily manipulated
Backs up words with actions	Angry
Always does the next right thing	Anxious
Is not manipulative and does not manipulate	Confused
Holds others accountable	Poor boundaries
Committed to doing what is right	Chaos
Respects individuality	Dominate and controlling
Harmonious	Passive and Double-minded
Teachable	Not interested in learning
Gentle	Prideful

> *If you expect mature devoted love, you must be a whole enough person to receive it.*

When you are working with immature people with lower levels of love, use your boundaries to choose loving responses. Do not mirror their behaviors, instead use your cognitive reasoning to resolve to love them by allowing them to experience their own suffering. Suffering, if we accept it, can work us through these stages at a faster pace.

APPENDIX B: UNSAFE VS. SAFE SELF

Introduction

- Our internal voice can be noisy.
- Learning to recognize your internal voice and take dominion over what it can say is a place of safety.
- Our world is not always safe or kind. However, we can always be kind to our self and others.
- This does not mean we are lazy, passive, or excuse makers.
- It is quite the opposite; we will develop intentional awareness of our thinking patterns that drive our anxiety.
- If you have anxiety and no internal voice, you probably have stomach issues and other chronic aches and pains. If you are a non-thinker, you will need a safe place and safe people to help trace the breadcrumbs back to the lies you believe that cause intense feelings of anxiety.

Lesson

Identify unsafe behaviors and intentionally develop safe behaviors.

Check the ones that apply to your inner self:	

Unsafe Inner Self An unsafe inner self:	
1) Starving for approval from others to validate yourself	
2) Gives in to peer pressure or conforms to expectations of others	
3) Self-abuse: alcohol, drugs, cutting, suicide thinking, etc.	
4) Self-destructive ("I do not care" attitude.)	
5) Abusive in relationships	
6) Sulky, broody, pouty, self-pity, whining	
7) Allows yourself to be abused	
8) Gives in to feelings of helplessness	
9) Feels worthless	
10) Attracts negative energy	
11) Stuck in a trauma cycle	
12) Lives with unresolved grief	
• Results: isolation, rejection, self-neglect, abandonment of duty, loneliness	

Safe Inner Self A safe inner self:	
1) Listens to feelings as a teacher but is not ruled by them	

2) Does not speak negatively or put yourself or others down	
3) Coaches yourself	
4) Is gracious and kind to yourself	
5) Gives grace to injuries and weakened parts of the body	
6) Finds a place of peace	
7) Is not easily provoked or out of balance	
8) Secure in who you are along your journey	
9) Can regulate emotional pain and rebalance quickly	
10) Follows a trusted path	
11) Develops good coping skills	
12) Develops community of trusted friends and acquaintances	
13) Practices humor	
14) Enjoys life	
• Results: peace and self-acceptance	

Exercise

Choose one thing that is unsafe, that burdens you that you want to stop doing and one thing that is safe that you want to work on today.

Application

Today, we will practice being safe for ourselves. This means you need to find things in the present to enjoy: a flower, a kitten, a child, a warm cup of tea, a soft pillow, a nice breeze, a sunny sky, etc.

Principle

Be humble and lay down your burdens to find rest for your soul (emotions).

Come to me, all you who are weary and burdened, and I will give you rest. Take my yoke upon you and learn from me, for I am gentle and humble in heart, and you will find rest for your souls. For my yoke is easy and my burden is light. Matthew 11:28-30

Conclusion

As I separate my identity from my unsafe self and loved ones with dysfunctional behaviors, I can develop a new identity of a safe self. I can know who I am and determine how much I will and will not tolerate from myself or others. Sometimes, I take myself by the scruff of the neck and shake myself and say, "you will stop that!". If I am stuck in a toxic environment, I can empower myself by developing a plan of escape. I always have choices. I may not like them, but I have choices.

The Lord is my Rock, and my fortress and my deliverer, my God, my strength, in whom I trust… Psalm 18:2

Prayer

O Lord help me to lay down my burdens and find rest for my soul (emotions). Mature me to be safe for myself and safe for others to love me and enjoy my company. Help me to consciously choose to walk in humility and gentleness every day. In Jesus Name, Amen.

Write out your prayer:

Start with O God,

APPENDIX C: DOMESTIC VIOLENCE

Once you break free and are triggered with any mention of the abuser's name empower yourself. Reprogram your subconscious with the strength of God's Word. **God is my protector. The Lord is my defender. The Lord will deliver me.**

Choose to trust God and not be afraid. Pray for this protection with a child-like faith. Lord, protect me, defend me, and deliver me from all my fears.

This does not mean that you do nothing. You get counsel from a domestic violence shelter and from their attorneys. You take out restraining orders or do anything else you need to do to protect yourself and your children or family.

The biggest power the old abuser has over you is fear. This fear invokes our minds with the memories of the abuse as if it is happening now. Your brain does not know that it isn't. Your body releases chemicals and goes into all the emotional memory of the past abuse.

It will take some awareness to be able to recognize the panic as an emotional memory and pull it up from your subconscious and remind yourself that you are safe and that it is not happening now. Tell yourself, "It's not happening now. I am safe. I can walk away."

Process what it was that attracted you to this person. Write out the excuses you made for them and then how they trigger you now and what you are going to do to empower yourself. Rehearse what you will or will not say if you are face to face with them. Rehearse how you might be able to de-escalate the situation if you needed to.

Often, if you just remove yourself from their line of sight and get out of their cross hairs, they abuse others and leave you alone.

APPENDIX D: SAMSON: SELF-ABSORPTION = BETRAYAL.

Lust and Anger are Siblings.

You can't have a healthy relationship built on lust. Lust and anger are siblings. Once the lust is enflamed and cannot be satisfied, the jealousy begins and fires up the anger and ends in destruction. The lust didn't build trust. Its turns on a fire that burns you both and destroys everything in its path.

Even if the relationship could move from lust to tender passion, to real and lasting love, it is so intense emotionally that it flares toxicity and not undying loyalty. This triggers fear bonds and self-preservation behaviors.

Samson was an Israelite called by God before his birth to be a judge of Israel and subdue the Philistine enemies. A Judge of Israel was to keep himself pure and his closest companions and his spouse were to be a follower of the one true God.

But, instead, Samson let his passions direct him and dictate his morality. He was careless with his anointing from God and lost his God given (stronger than a 1,000 men) strength. Samson's strength made him arrogant and this self-absorption attitude of "I get what I want" eventually rendered him weak as any man, blind and in captivity.

Samson was powerless over his lustful appetites. Continually, he indulged in relationships with women who betrayed him. Samson fulfilled his call to subdue the Philistines and did so for 40 years, but not out of his love for God. He only answered his call when he was personally irritated, and he paid the price for it. *Read the story in Judges 14-16*

Self-absorption attracts betrayal.

Jumping Ditches

If you leave a one broken relationship who is unable to nurture you, be careful that you don't end up with a person who can nurture you momentarily but without stability to sustain the relationship. You may just be jumping from one ditch to another and land in the exact same place or worse.

APPENDIX E: PROVERBS 7: THE SEDUCER

Seductress/Seducer
• Attire of a harlot
• loud
• stubborn
• feet don't stay home.
• in the streets
• seducing
• pursuing
• fair speech

We can be a seducer/seductress or be seduced through naivety. When we are wounded and indulge improper attention seeking behaviors, we develop patterns of selfishness and end up devouring others.

Lure of a simpleton
• Void of understanding
• Hates instruction.
• Despised reproof
• Going astray
• Sluggard
• Froward mouth
• Following folly
• Enticed/seduced.

• Held in the chords of sin.
• On the path to hell
• To the chambers of death

A simpleton is someone without goals and direction in life and just goes with whatever is in front of them. They are easily led astray onto the wrong path. In a sex crazed culture, sex looks normal and like pleasure that will satisfy but it does not. Repetitive patterns of sexual indulges with multiple partners will feed all other addictive behaviors and trigger a whole host of trauma wounds and immature inner core responses. Relationship recovery must be as intentional as substance use recovery. Emotional recovery must also be growing through character and practicing the fruit of the Spirit.

Consequences for Immorality
• Dishonor
• Strangers have wealth.
• Mourn
• Our sin binds us.
• Gone astray.
• Brought to a piece of bread.
• Burned

• Destroyed soul.
• Wounded
• Reproach
• Led to the slaughter.
• Ends in death.

If you have relationship addictions and get burned repeatedly, read these verses often. Then as you grow in a desire to maintain sexual sobriety work God's sexual sobriety plan. If you start a relationship and want to dominate or control the person, you just triggered a bunch of junk. Back up and wait.

You can pray for a healthy relationship. It must start slowly and with intentionality and a lot of accountabilities.

God's Sexual Sobriety Instruction
1. Pay attention to wisdom.
2. Listen for instructions.
3. Depart not from God's Word
4. Don't go near sin.
5. Receive instruction/reproof.
6. Obey your teachers.
7. Keep commandments!
8. Bind commandments on your heart.
9. Tie them about thy neck.
10. Lust not.

11. Don't look!

Proverbs 4:20-27 NIV

My son, pay attention to what I say; turn your ear to my words. [21] Do not let them out of your sight, keep them within your heart; [22] for they are life to those who find them and health to one's whole body. [23] Above all else, guard your heart, for everything you do flows from it. [24] Keep your mouth free of perversity; keep corrupt talk far from your lips. [25] Let your eyes look straight ahead; fix your gaze directly before you. [26] Give careful thought to the paths for your feet and be steadfast in all your ways. [27] Do not turn to the right or the left; keep your foot from evil.

Proverbs 5:1-23 NIV

My son, pay attention to my wisdom, turn your ear to my words of insight, [2] that you may maintain discretion and your lips may preserve knowledge. [3] For the lips of the adulterous woman drip honey, and her speech is smoother than oil; [4] but in the end she is bitter as gall, sharp as a double-edged sword. [5] Her feet go down to death; her steps lead straight to the grave. [6] She gives no thought to the way of life; her paths wander aimlessly, but she does not know it. [7] Now then, my sons, listen to me; do not turn aside from what I say. [8] Keep to a path far from her, do not go near the door of her house, [9] lest you lose your honor to others and your dignity to one who is cruel, [10] lest strangers feast on your wealth and your toil enrich the house of another. [11] At the end of your life you will groan when your flesh and body are spent. [12] You will say, "How I hated discipline! How my heart spurned correction! [13] I would not obey my teachers or turn my ear to my instructors. [14] And I was soon in serious trouble in the assembly of God's people." [15] Drink water from your own cistern, running water from your own well. [16] Should your springs overflow in the streets, your streams of water in the public squares? [17] Let them be yours alone, never to be shared with strangers. [18] May your fountain be blessed, and may you rejoice in the wife of your youth. [19] A loving doe, a graceful deer-may her breasts satisfy you always, may you ever be intoxicated with her love. [20] Why, my son, be intoxicated with another man's wife? Why embrace the bosom of a wayward woman? [21] For your ways are in full view of the LORD, and he examines all your paths. [22] The evil deeds of the wicked ensnare them; the cords of their sins hold them fast. [23] For lack of discipline they will die, led astray by their own great folly.

Proverbs 6:20-35 NIV

My son, keep your father's command and do not forsake your mother's teaching. [21] Bind them always on your heart; fasten them around your neck. [22] When you walk, they will guide you; when you sleep, they will watch over you; when you awake, they will speak to you. [23] For this command is a lamp, this teaching is a light, and correction and instruction are the way to life, [24] keeping you from your neighbor's wife, from the smooth talk of a wayward woman. [25] Do not lust in your heart after her beauty or let her captivate you with her eyes. [26] For a prostitute can be had for a loaf of bread, but another man's wife preys on your very life. [27] Can a man scoop fire into his lap without his clothes being burned? [28] Can a man walk on hot coals without his feet being scorched? [29] So is he who sleeps with another man's wife; no one who touches her will go unpunished. [30] People do not despise a thief if he steals to satisfy his hunger when he is starving. [31] Yet if he is caught, he must pay sevenfold, though it costs him all the wealth of his house. [32] But a man who commits adultery has no sense; whoever does so destroys himself. [33] Blows and disgrace are his lot, and his shame will never be wiped away. [34] For jealousy arouses a husband's fury, and he will show no mercy when he takes revenge. [35] He will not accept any compensation; he will refuse a bribe; however great it is.

Proverbs 7:1-27 NIV
My son, keep my words and store up my commands within you. [2] Keep my commands and you will live; guard my teachings as the apple of your eye. [3] Bind them on your fingers; write them on the tablet of your heart. [4] Say to wisdom, "You are my sister," and to insight, "You are my relative." [5] They will keep you from the adulterous woman, from the wayward woman with her seductive words. [6] At the window of my house I looked down through the lattice. [7] I saw among the simple, I noticed among the young men,

a youth who had no sense. [8] He was going down the street near her corner, walking along in the direction of her house [9] at twilight, as the day was fading, as the dark of night set in. [10] Then out came a woman to meet him, dressed like a prostitute and with crafty intent. [11] (She is unruly and defiant, her feet never stay at home; [12] now in the street, now in the squares, at every corner she lurks.) [13] She took hold of him and kissed him and with a brazen face she said: [14] "Today I fulfilled my vows, and I have food from my fellowship offering at home. [15] So I came out to meet you; I looked for you and have found you! [16] I have covered my bed with colored linens from Egypt. [17] I have perfumed my bed with myrrh, aloes, and cinnamon. [18] Come, let's drink deeply of love till morning; let's enjoy ourselves with love! [19] My husband is not at home; he has gone on a long journey. [20] He took his purse filled with money and will not be home till full moon." [21] With persuasive words she led him astray; she seduced him with her smooth talk. [22] All at once he followed her like an ox going to the slaughter, like a deer stepping into a noose [23] till an arrow pierces his liver, like a bird darting into a snare, little knowing it will cost him his life. [24] Now then, my sons, listen to me; pay attention to what I say. [25] Do not let your heart turn to her ways or stray into her paths. [26] Many are the victims she has brought down; her slain are a mighty throng. [27] Her house is a highway to the grave, leading down to the chambers of death.

Impotency

Remember not to elevate sexual function to a level of identity. Sex is pleasurable and fun and makes you feel whole and complete. Let's face it, orgasm turns the world right side up for a moment. But love making can be done with impotency. Love is full of eye contact and heart connection. It is stroking, hugging, kissing, whispers, and soft murmurings of teasing.

A being seen and heard and the center of attention without a care in the world. A moment without time. It is forgetting all that burdens or robs peace. It is deep and satisfying breaths of oneness. It's all about you. Oh wait! It all about me. No wait! It's all about unity. A fullness of the hearts connected that forgets the problems of yesterday or the troubles of tomorrow.

You know… it gives the strength and courage to persevere through struggles. Just knowing you are loved and knowing your value stops the storms inside.

I think that if mature love is nothing and yet it is everything… If it is giving and receiving… If it is without expectation or confinement… If it is free to come and to go… If it is always present… If it is always safe… If it can be broken and mended quickly… If it can be held safely in a burning heart. Romance is the true connection of the hearts.

Impotency can be survived if you don't disconnect your heart. It is the identification with the shame that makes you hide and forget who you are. You are so much more.

Unless, of course, you struggle with connection and sex is the only way you know how to connect. If so, you need to move towards connection in communication, and eye contact and playing with her hair and stroking her back. The period of impotency whether it be short or long can make you more sensitive to feeling with your heart and finding your value in true intimacy and connection. This period, however short or long, if embraced, can give you a whole new set of values. It can make you tender and compassionate. It can bring out a nurturing gentle side of you.

So, in conclusion, be grateful for impotency. It can, if you let it, open a whole world of gentleness towards yourself and your lover. The deep and rich heart connection can always survive the test of time. The beastly, somewhat selfish, let me get off man will be frustrated, aggravated, withdrawn and hide in shame or the gentle man will emerge and become a devoted, faithful lover. A lover of her soul.

Think about it. If you cannot sexually perform, you will have to perform emotionally. This, for you, can be uncomfortable if you have only seen women as sexual pleasure for you. Or if your identity as a man is in your sexual function. But now this woman can be more than sex. She can be a best friend, confidant, and intimately connected to you in a deeper way.

Or you can run, hide, and make your job or hobby your lover and push her away. This may give you an allusion of control, but it will destroy your relationship quickly.

You can embrace shame and think you are less of a man. But that's a lie too. Did you not know that she gave you sex for the pleasure of your closeness? She likes to be held as much or more than the act of sex. It is the closeness to you and the physical touch that conceives intimacy and fullness in her soul.

JOURNAL PROMPTS

1. O Lord, can I recover a relationship with you. One where I talk to you and come to you and meditate on your word and you hear, see, comfort, guide and strengthen me. Lord, I understand the necessities of the suffering and the relationship struggles to make me depend upon you more. Will you comfort me now? Listen and write comforting words to yourself.

2. Lord, I feel like I am dragging my feet. How do I redeem the time? The work is too great for me. I need more strength. I need a supernatural immune system, a strong stable mind, and a healthy body. Lord, help me serve you day and night. What do I need to do to grow and mature?

3. Your Word says you are GOD, and you will calm the storm in me? Will you fill my heart with your love and give me peace? It's so uncomfortable in my skin. It's painful. It's sad. It's lonely. It's empty. It's rejected. It's accused. Help me to remember who I am in you. Help me not faint!
Write out the good things God says about you?

4. I don't have a friend for me. I don't have a counselor or mentor. My thinking is being skewed towards the world. My mouth is being perverted to swearing. I need a faithful friend to come along side me that doesn't murmur or ramble but has godly wisdom. A friend from God that will cherish and not judge me. One that won't treat me like I am crazy or in the way or refuse me when I reach. again. What would it look like if I became my own best friend and counseled myself with God's Word?

5. I pray Lord that you would give me a huge token of your favor today that I would know for sure you loved me. Help the sick version of me to heal. What emotional sickness keeps you stuck?

6. Cleanse me of a guilty conscience. Take not your Holy Spirit from me. Shape me and mold me into your image. Agreeing with shame, guilt and self-condemnation keeps me stuck. Agreeing with the finished work of Christ empowers me to receive his love and move forward. What guilt and shame do I once and for all need to release?

7. Lord, would you help me to laugh again. Let me hear myself laugh. Help me to let go of the pain of the past so I can move forward. I give you permission to laugh and enjoy your day.

PRAYERS

1. Be with me today. Show me your favor. Provide for me in such a magnificent way that I know I belong to you. Lord, let me pray and you answer. Let me be so close you to that I can hear your heartbeat and feel your breath upon my face. Let my heart burn for you as it has in the past. Clear my anxiety. Cleanse my confusion. Deliver me from all evil. Set me above and not beneath. Make me the head and not the tail. Show me that my work is not in vain.

2. Could you burn in worship in my heart? Show me what pleases you. Show me how to be a lover of you again. Refresh me. Refresh my soul. Draw near me and comfort me with your love that will hold me through the pain of the night. Give me your secrets. Give me focus.

3. *My friend,*
   May you praise God in all your affliction and distress.
   May you embrace your earthquake and let it break the shackles that bind you.
   May the quake shake the foundation of the false beliefs that bind you.

May it break open the prison doors of lies that holds you.
And may you sing and worship to the glory of God. Amen
Wait on the Lord, I say wait!
And he will strengthen you with his righteous right hand.
He will give you the desires of your heart.

DEVOTIONS

Feeling Unloved

It isn't that we need to love others more and give them more access to our hearts. We can't demand to be loved. We can set up boundaries and demand to be respected, but not loved. So, we will still feel unloved. The demand for the need of love will just push others away.

When others can't fill our need to be loved it will just feel like they hold us at arm's length. No matter how hard we try, we will still fee unloved. This feeling may have come from being unwanted as a child. This wound is hard to heal.

About ten years ago, things flipped upside down and my heart got repeatedly stabbed. Since then, I have not been able to feel the love of God the same way. I have not felt like I was precious to God anymore.

It's like I envision God only having a drop of love for me if I do what he wants. Throwing me another job and another job. I saw in a prayer vision evil pulling me apart in a dozen ways.

Before this time, I spent a decade with my heart burning every morning with God's love for me.

Somehow, I have felt rejected by God and not ever able to do enough. Like I am annoying and in the way. That's not God's feelings towards me, it is my perception because of the mistreatment of others.

The key to this next step of my healing is to separate people from myself enough that they aren't my source. Only God is my source of love and complete acceptance.

This is higher level maturity. This is taking back my power. This is returning to the Lord in such a way that no circumstance and no person can rob me of my love for God and his love for me.

It's a fake perception anyway. Coming from a wounded heart and unmet expectations.

Assignment:

Open your heart to the Lord.

Pray for the spiritual maturity skill of Self-Actualization. When I am fully mature, I will be able to carry the presence of the Lord always. I will carry kindness, empathy, and compassion. I will be peaceful and able to self-regulate quickly if I get out of balance. This is the goal of maturity.

Navigating Emotional Landmines

May you be strong enough to ebb and flow through life. Practice grace and patience for yourself. Recognizing your trauma wounds stopped your emotional growth. If you had Attention Deficit medications as a child, or developed substance use disorder at a young age or were molested you are stunted emotionally.

Learn to flip scenarios and look at every circumstance as learning ground to develop healthy emotional skills to navigate life. Feel it in little bites or determine to feel it later just like Scarlett

O'Hare in the movie "Gone with the Wind". The devastation of the Civil War should have consumed Scarlet. Instead, she just determined to do the next right thing for survival.

Manners

Mind your manners. Manners can go a long way to reducing stress and developing safe relationships. Don't be a sponge but instead, own your own emotions. Decide which emotions you will indulge and how long you will feel them.

Recognize the physical responses to trauma wounds in your exaggerated reactions to a circumstance. Sit and breathe through any emotion that is overwhelming and regulate yourself to a place of calm before you interact with anyone.

Healthy Love

The relationship can only be healthy when there are **no expectations**. You are ok with not knowing if the other will ever return. You can **stay in the present** and **enjoy your day**. You allow the other person the **freedom to come, stay or go.**

You allow the other person to choose what is best for themselves with **no pressure.** You are **emotionally mature** enough to not get entangled in rejection, abandonment, and neglect issues if the person decides to go.

What if you can take what you need and leave the rest? It could be a stress-free safe zone. It must be always **giving and gently receiving** but never dominance or control.

Song of Solomon

May your heart burn with a lover like the Song of Solomon. Let your heart be protected until you are safe to be open to love.

Deep inside of a wounded heart, there may be a part that has died and grieved every day. When you mend a torn heart, you will find a part that was gone. The secret is that **within yourself you have all that you need.**

Love shares

Friends or lovers? Friends comfort and connect. Friends listen to your hurts and help you heal.

Lovers share everything. They share likes and dislikes, thoughts, feelings, moods, touch, hugs, kisses, snuggles, and backrubs. Warm hearts. Warm thoughts. Even rainy days are sunny.

Sabotage

If you find love and then sabotage your happiness, identify your insecurities and the lies you believe about your worth.

Next, build a trust muscle. Trusting you can be strong with or without your lover.

Your **emotional stability is within yourself**. Your strength is yours to give or to take back. Do not abandon yourself.

Thriving on Connection

There is a blessed connectedness with friends where you can just be yourself. There is a carefree conversation without judgment. Your heart is known, and you are heard and valued.

Acts of kindness and gentleness makes us feel valued. Even a baby will struggle to thrive and develop without physical touch. Make sure you have safe touch and lots of hugs with friends.

Healthy Sex

Healthy sex reattaches you to your body and your partner. Love gives you a spiritual connection to another. It is a place of safety. The physical act of sex makes you present in the moment and gives you a feeling of connectedness and security. This must be reserved for a special person or will be cheapened and leave many scars.

Single

Physical exercise or movement connects you to yourself. It is important if you are single to reconnect frequently to your breath and stay present in the moment. Learning to trust yourself means you will not divide with anxiety. Journal your feelings and process them. Feel all your feelings quickly and move through them by detaching from them and releasing them and replace them with words of affirmation and self-love.

I lay my strong emotions, particularly my sorrows on the altar as my sacrifice for the day. I must learn to speak to myself kindly and coach myself with love.

Self-talk is extremely important. Release your desire for a relationship with another and develop a strong trusting relationship with yourself. Learn to be a strong decision maker and develop a strong sense of your own self-worth.

Refuse guilt, shame, and self-condemnation.

Don't force yourself to feel guilty because of a religious spirit that says we cannot or shall not. *Let no man therefore judge you in meat, or in drink, or in respect of a holyday, or of the new moon, or of the sabbath days.*

Wherefore if ye be dead with Christ from the rudiments of the world, why as though living in the world, are ye subject to ordinances, Touch not: taste not; handle not: Which all are to perish with the using; after the commandments and doctrines of men? Which things have indeed a show of wisdom in will worship, and humility, and neglecting of the body, not in any honor to the satisfying of the flesh? Colossians 2:16-23

Reconnecting to your source

So, the real issue is reconnecting to you. I give you my heart again and fully trust you, my Lord. Here is an outline of my journal entry as I cast off the rejection and strengthen my identity in the Lord. If I don't know what makes me suffer, I can't move it out of myself and then the suffering or rejection becomes part of my identity. I think the Lord is strong enough to hear my complaints and remind me he is near.

1) My trust in you has been eroded by men.

2) My heart has been fully shot up with rejection.

3) My confidence has been stripped.

4) The emotional abuse of neglect has given me a cancer of helplessness.

5) My identity as a wife and mother has been stripped.

6) I can't remember who I was.

7) I don't know who I am now.

8) Surely, I am a wife who is abandoned and unloved.

When I am with you Lord:

1) I am not a broken woman, but strong and mighty in Spirit.

2) I am not a woman shunned but accepted through Christ.

3) I am not rejected. You are a father to the orphans. You are a husband to the widow.

4) I am not denied your love. I am loved with an everlasting love.

5) I am not hopeless, helpless, or confused but empowered through the hope that you place with me.

Healthy relationship feelings…

1) Blessed
2) Hopeful

3) Whole, complete, safe, seen and loved.
4) Warm from kisses and big hugs
5) Thriving with connectedness
6) Emotionally attuned and regulated.
7) Feeling safe and loved.

Grace 1

And, by your grace, I will keep my eyes on you. Will you be my lover, Lord? Will you stop the spirit of Rachal lamenting and weeping and refusing to be comforted? Will you comfort, bless, heal, redeem, cleanse, and deliver? Let me distance myself from sorrow and confusion. Many of us are so broken, that we refuse comfort. Today comfort yourself and receive comfort from others.

Grace 2

This is the age of grace. It doesn't mean we can go into darkness and find light. It means when we are stumbling and staggering, we have a Savior that is still for us. There is no mistake that could remove you from his love. Nothing that would cause the Lord to shame or reject you. When the door is always open, it isn't a forced union or a ball and chain marriage you are stuck in. It is a loving wooing. A gentle kindness and pursuing of your heart. There is a love of God that is powerful and intimate if you will just receive.

Romans 8:37-39 NIV

No, in all these things we are more than conquerors through him who loved us. [38] For I am convinced that neither death nor life, neither angels nor demons, neither the present nor the future, nor any powers, [39] neither height nor depth, nor anything else in all creation, will be able to separate us from the love of God that is in Christ Jesus our Lord.

Grieving

Well, the grieving won't stop until you stop giving yourself away to someone who is emotionally unavailable. If he loved you, he would be here. He would not be content without you. Be careful to not repeat your past. Sick girl thinks she will get fullness of embrace, affection, and love. And instead gets obsessing, lust, and avoidance. You may just be repeating your past. What do you want me to learn Lord?

Let my heart softened towards you, my Lord, open my heart to love again.

Religious Spirit tells us we are unworthy.

The religious spirits of today tell us we aren't worthy. One sin is met with rejection and maybe even makes me an outcast.

There is a childlike innocence where we can always return to the father and find an unconditional love. Let the Spirit of the Lord guide you into his love. Where the door is open. You will never feel suffocated or controlled. There will never be a demand to perform or be someone you aren't. You can take off your mask and just be you.

You will have the tenderness of Jesus, the pursuing lover, that delights in you. This delight doesn't ever have to end. There is no shutting you out or shutting you down. There is no avoidance or impatience. There is no bullying and controlling.

Where the Spirit of the Lord is there, there is liberty. This liberty is freedom to love and move in your true self.

2 Corinthians 3:17 NIV

Now the Lord is the Spirit, and where the Spirit of the Lord is, there is freedom.

Small Group
Mentors Guide

This curriculum will bring quick insight into the heart of believers and will give them tools to evaluate their internal conflict, find the source of the confusion and help them correct their thinking.

It would be optimal for those who are new in recovery to have a mentor or a small group to do the studies with them until they can confidently find the Scriptures and answer the questions. Thinking principles could also be discussed in a group meeting, where the focus is on truth and **not** social issues.

Do not force anyone to participate early on. Let them soak up the information and have some time to process it. Let them find safety to explore their inner wounds. Love them through this process.

Think of others as wounded soldiers who need nurtured and given time to heal. As they grow, they will be prepared to fight for their freedom through the power of the Living Word.

Conclusion

For God did not give us a spirit of timidity (fear), but a spirit of power, of love and of self-discipline (sound mind). 2 Timothy 1:7 Could this mean that a sound mind comes from self-discipline. The Scriptures used are the NIV unless otherwise noted. The words in parenthesis are used from the KJV for emphasis or clarification.

Moderators

1. Open in prayer.
2. Review Group Rules.
3. Review last week's lesson. Ask how they were able to apply it to their life and any success or failures they experienced.
4. Do the audio presentation (YouTube video/Angie G Meadows; or Podcast audio/Rock of Recovery) or teach your own presentation using the material.
5. Go through the lesson one point at a time for open discussion.
6. If group is over 8-12 members, split it up into smaller groups for discussion. Train your stronger believers for co-leader support positions.
7. Give examples of how God helped you solve the problem.
8. End the group in prayer (Take prayer request or have a basket for them to write out written request and ask them to mark the request "private" or "public").
9. If time allows, add an opportunity for those with heavy burdens to stay longer for encouragement and prayer.

Small Group Rules

1. Give everyone an opportunity to speak.
2. Keep the discussion to the topic.
3. We are not here to "fix" each other. We are here to support and encourage one another.
4. If you do not want to share, simply say "pass" when it comes to your turn.
5. It is vital that this is a safe place for everyone. No negative, judgmental, or condemning comments. The Rule is LOVE!
6. Confidentiality is mandatory and is taken very seriously.
7. Whatever is spoken in this room, stays in this room.
8. If during the week, you discuss another member's comments among one another, it is to be in the spirit of prayer and encouragement and not in mockery or ridicule. No gossiping or slandering will be tolerated.
9. There will be a release of anyone who wants to leave after the lesson and discussion time.
10. There will often be added extra time of sharing at the end of the group for those with heavy burdens who want to share their struggles and receive individual prayer or for those who want to stay and encourage those struggling.

LEADERSHIP GUIDELINES

Dishonorable Leadership	Honorable Leadership
Anger	Happy Countenance
Use of fear tactics	Approachable
Threats/Bullying	Patient and Kind
Retaliation for being confronted	Gracious; holds others accountable
Hasty/Rash	Treats everyone the same
Impatient	Good self-identity
Arrogant	Good boundaries
Values self, money, or project goals more than people	Good mentors Good relationships
Holds a grudge	Unemotional decision maker
Plays favorites	Leads through serving
Casts confusion on situations to blame shift	Humble- Leads with service and under submission to their authority
Makes emotional decisions not principally based decisions	Will do what is right, no matter the consequences
Denies problems	Good listener
Deals only with superficial problems	Forgives easily, coaches weaker ones; encourages.

	others.
Ignores the main problem	Identifies root problems
Does not seek counsel	Seeks many counselors
Ask impossible unrealistic things from subordinates	Able to plan and develop goals
Demanding/Unreasonable	Able to follow through with a plan
Nebuchadnezzar the pagan king in the book of Daniel.	Always same level of emotional availability *Adapted from observation of the behaviors of Daniel and

Rules: No bullying or verbal abuse ever!

Kind, patient but sometimes very firm.

GOOD FOLLOWER

1. Respects Authority
2. Protects Good Name
3. Learns to Stand Alone (not follow a crowd)
4. Guards the truth.
5. Takes responsibility for actions.
6. Honorable and fair in decisions.
7. Makes good sound financial decisions.
8. Lives with Self-Control
9. Moderation in all things
10. Gives good days work without complaint.
11. Always on time; dependable
12. Never gossips, slanders, or accuses.
13. Takes any issues up the ladder through the chain of command.
14. Guards all that is entrusted into their hands; trustworthy.
15. Refuses to do anything illegal, unethical, or immoral.

*You must learn to be a good follower to be a good leader.

Author's Biography

Angie Meadows is passionate to help families develop healthy relationships, reconcile, and heal. She graduated from St Mary's School of Nursing as a Registered Nurse, Marshall University with a bachelor's in nursing and Ohio State University with a master's in nursing. She volunteers in the recovery community in multiple capacities and works one on one with family members and those in active recovery. She is currently a grandmother, wife, mother, speaker, and writer. Her favourite past time is writing and quilting.

OTHER RESOURCES BY THE AUTHOR

A Thousand Tears: An Enabler's Journey: Meadows RN, MS, Angie G., Meadows MD, JD, Perry, Meadows BS, Sarah J.: 9781732810204: Amazon.com: Books

ISBN 9781732810204

This is the same book as Enabler's Journey: A Christian Perspective, but it is written with principles and not Scriptures.

The book identifies the Enabler's Cycle and our conflict with individuals with addiction. Identifying manipulative, devouring, or toxic relationships in our life and learning to confront and detach. It also includes multiple self-assessment tools: Enabler's paradigm, entanglement gauge, anxiety quotient, trust scales, and much more.

An Enabler's Journey: A Christian Perspective: Meadows RN, MS, Angie G., Meadows MD, JD, Perry, Meadows BS, Sarah J.: 9781732810211: Amazon.com: Books

ISBN: 9781732810211

This book is 300+ pages and 24 chapters. It is almost the same book as *A Thousand Tear: An Enabler's Journey* except it has a 100+ Scriptures to validate the principles for dealing with difficult people in relationships. This book will convince the elderly Christian family members to stop enabling.

Enabler's Journey Recovery Plan: Enabler's Journey Recovery Series: Book 1: Angie G. Meadows, Meadows MD, JD,

Perry, Meadows BS, Sarah: 9781732810228: Amazon.com: Books

ISBN: 9781732810228

This is a 100+ page Book One of a recovery workbook series. It guides individuals and clients to understand enabling behaviours and evaluate their current participation in perpetuating a person with substance use disorder's illness. The enabler will learn to recognize the cycle of enabling, entanglement, excuses, and beliefs that handicap an enabler from recovery. It also coaches in the courage needed for detaching from destructive people and circumstances we cannot control. The book includes an enabler's recovery plan, accountability questionnaire, self-care program and a plan for identifying unhealthy and healthy coping strategies. It will also guide the recovering enabler to determine a level of safe involvement with a person with substance use disorder and how to identify true and false recovery, rebuild trust, and avoid the snare of another enabling relationship. It will help us recognize dysfunctional thinking and our false belief system that keeps us entangled. There are 5 chapters from the original *A Thousand Tears: An Enabler's Journey* book and 3 extra in-depth recovery chapters and many added self-evaluation charts. This is a beginner book or small group book for an Enablers. It is short and concise with lots of diagrams and easy to understand flowcharts. It is a great beginner tool with lots of reflective questions for counsellors or small groups to use in guiding enablers to recovery.

Enabler's Journey Detachment: Enabler's Journey Recovery Series Book 2: Meadows RN, MS, Angie G, Meadows MD, JD,

Perry, Meadows BS, Sarah: 9781732810235: Amazon.com: Books
ISBN: 9781732810235

This book empowers us to learn survival skills with 12 DETACHMENT PRINCIPLES. The spiralling financial consequences, mental anguish, emotional chaos, and physical drain of enabling begs the voice of detachment to ensure self-preservation. This book is a useful tool in dealing with substance use disorder, or other individuals with abusive or irresponsible behaviours. It includes many self-assessment tools: Entitlement Evaluation, Empowerment Plan, Helpless Trap, Healthier Me, Healthy Speech Evaluation, Negative Emotional Triggers, Unmet Needs, Obsessive Thinking Traps, Forgiveness, Bitterness, Reconciliation, Holidays, Suffering, Power to Stop Enabling, Self-Talk, Rules for Survival, practical steps, reflective thinking and much, much more.

Rock of Recovery Anxiety Trap: Christian Enabler/Addiction Recovery: Meadows MSN, RN, Angie G, Meadows BS, Sarah J: 9781732810242: Amazon.com: Books
ISBN:9781732810242

Painful emotions drive toxic relationships and addictive behaviors. Developmental emotional maturity skills mimic physical developmental skills. As a child grows physically, they learn to roll over, sit up, crawl, walk and then run. The development of emotions can be stunted or undeveloped and need to be matured and nurtured through intentional training and disciplining our intellect and thinking to support, nurture and master our emotions. Conquering anxiety, finding a safe self internally, learning to break a helpless/victim trap with disciplined thinking, uncovering hidden emotions under the cloak of anxiety, overcoming doublemindedness, and internally finding rest and peace are just a few developmental emotional skills to rule and reign over our internal world.

Amazon.com: Rule and Reign Your Internal World: Defeating Anxiety: 9781732810259: Meadows MSN RN, Angie G, Meadows BS, Sarah J: Books **ISBN:9781732810259**

This is the same information as the Rock of Recovery Series for Enablers and those with substance use disorder. It is reorganized for anyone needing Developmental Emotional Maturity Skills. This series is an individual devotional, home-school, or Christian School curriculum, Family Devotions, or Small Group anxiety study. Ages 14 and above.

Rock of Recovery Overcoming Torment: Christian Enabler/Addiction Recovery: Meadows MSN RN, Angie G, Meadows BS, Sarah J: 9781732810266: Amazon.com: Books **ISBN 9781732810266**

Unresolved anxiety can become passive tormented thinking, which ends with trauma. Now, let us unravel these dysfunctional thinking patterns and gain emotional maturity. This book teaches us to recognize trauma, its triggers, inner core emotional responses and its severe behavioral responses along with accompanying mental prisons and mind control holding us captive. We will learn to draw these traumas into our conscious thinking and intentionally reprogram them by practicing character skills and healthy responses. The book includes: a mental torment evaluation, spiritual maturity skills, thought test scale, mental torment scale, signs and symptoms of spiritual sickness, sign of spiritual health, how to stop an offense, types of offenses, who needs a boundary, reasons to avoid an offense, a yoke of slavery, wound identifier with its emotional responses, bitterness, characteristics of depression, reframing a wound, drunk vs. sober emotions, emotional movement quiz, and forgiveness steps with cautions. This is the second book in the Rock of Recovery Series.

Rule and Reign Your Internal World Overcoming Torment
https://www.amazon.com/Reign-Internal-World-Overcoming-Torment/dp/B0C2RM939D/ref=sr_1_1?crid=2XX53GIIWEUBM&keywords=Rule+and+Reign+Your+Internal+World+Overcoming+Torment&qid=1689616117&s=books&sprefix=rule+and+reign+your+internal+world+overcoming+torment%2Cstripbooks%2C104&sr=1-1

This is the same information as the Rock of Recovery Overcoming Torment for Enablers and those with substance use disorder. It is reorganized for anyone needing Developmental Emotional Maturity Skills. This series is an individual devotional, home-school, or Christian School curriculum, Family Devotions, or Small Group anxiety study. Ages 14 and above.

Rock of Recovery Overcoming Trauma: Christian Enabler/Addiction Recovery: Meadows, Angie G: 9781732810273: Amazon.com: Books **ISBN:9781732810273**

In this book we learn how to identify our trauma wounds and inner core responses and recognize, release, and retrain our emotions. There will be a trauma trap evaluation, a mood tracer, understanding mental prisons, mind control, a higher ground emotional trainer, thought regulator, understanding healthy love, finding joy, peace, patience, gentleness, spiritual sickness, feeble vs. healthy faith, and finding freedom in self-control. Emotional maturity identifies and heals our inner wounds to bring lasting recovery. Without the emotional skills to navigate trauma, substance use disorder and/or habitually immature core thinking patterns will perpetuate the suffering of inner chaos.

Rock of Recovery Spirit and Soul Disconnect

https://www.amazon.com/Rock-Recovery-Spirit-Soul-Disconnect/dp/1732810281/ref=sr_1_1?crid=1RYTPK2WGFV60&keywords=Rock+of+Recovery+Spirit+and+Soul+Disconnect&qid=1678733388&sprefix=rock+of+recovery+spirit+and+soul+disconnect%2Caps%2C94&sr=8-1

Rock of Recovery Spirit and Soul Disconnect. Anything that causes you suffering, or anxiety is a disconnect. I disconnect from my true self and connect to anxiety and other emotional

suffering. This causes me to abandon my own self. Lessons include understanding your spirit, soul, emotional regression, root of depression, undisciplined thinking, immature conscience, trial of rejection, conquering oppression, understanding defilement, finding balance, steadfast vs faintheartedness, and learning to suffer well. There are guidelines for small groups, devotions, and Bible Studies.

Rock of Recovery Reconciliation

https://www.amazon.com/Rock-Recovery-Reconciliation-Addiction-Handbook/dp/B0BR6YC5PH/ref=sr_1_1?crid=3CAT02WDD348E&keywords=Rock+of+Recovery+Reconciliation&qid=1678733627&sprefix=rock+of+recovery+reconciliation%2Caps%2C94&sr=8-1

Rock of Recovery Reconciliation This book is specifically written for families to reconcile with loved ones returning from addiction recovery programs or prison. There are multiple outlines to discuss expectations, boundaries, empowerment plan, and goal setting. More evaluation scales are identifying active vs passive recovery, functional vs severe addiction, healthy speech, trust scale, victim boundaries, accountability, identifying lies, survival rules, dangerous behavior guidelines. This plan could be used by families or another third-party accountability partner for enablers and those in recovery or returning home after incarceration.

Seven Pillars of Wisdom

https://www.amazon.com/s?k=Angie+Meadows+ISBN+9781732810297&crid=1CVB3LADNK71J&sprefix=angie+meadows+isbn+9781732810297%2Caps%2C90&ref=nb_sb_noss

ISBN: 9781732810297

Seven Pillars of Wisdom. Wisdom has built her house; she has hewn out its seven pillars. This is a verse-by-verse study from Proverbs. The fear of the Lord is wisdom: understanding, discernment, truth, righteousness, knowledge, instruction, and prudence. These words will be thoroughly studied. This is an individual, small group Sunday School, Christian school Bible full semester Bible Study with multiple challenges at the end to develop your own studies and to mine for great treasures from the Word of God. Ages 13 and above.

Rock of Recovery Detachment

https://www.amazon.com/Rock-Recovery-Detachment-Christian-Addiction/dp/B0BYBKVD4J/ref=sr_1_1?crid=31DDG765FOCR3&keywords=Rock+of+Recovery+Detachment&qid=1689616029&s=books&sprefix=rock+of+recovery+detachment%2Cstripbooks%2C104&sr=1-1

ISBN: 979898429013

This book teaches the 12 Detachment Principles throughout Scripture to develop a healthy identity and healthy boundaries.

Principles #1 include Detachment is not cold, withdrawn, or isolated. Principle #2 Detachment is not caring less but caring more for my sanity. Principle #3 Detachment is understanding my emotional stability is not dependent on another person's sobriety.

The Daniel Study

https://www.amazon.com/Daniel-Study-Family-children-study/dp/B0C6BQ5CFN/ref=sr_1_1?crid=JH2MGMRJZ4NS&keywords=The+Daniel+Study+Angie+Meadows&qid=1689616069&s=books&sprefix=the+daniel+study+angie+meadows%2Cstripbooks%2C97&sr=1-1

ISBN:9798987429037

This book has the first 6 chapters of Daniel come alive for studies while studying the character skill that Daniel and his three friends needed to overcome their troubles. Each lesson has thinking principle, character skill, ten or more questions for the student to answer, self-evaluation section for applying what we are learning and a parent/teacher suggestion section. Ages 7 and above. A great beginner Bible study for any new Christian.

Kindle eBooks available for all title.

JOURNAL NOTES

www.ingramcontent.com/pod-product-compliance
Lightning Source LLC
Chambersburg PA
CBHW062042080426
42734CB00012B/2533

* 9 7 9 8 9 8 7 4 2 9 0 4 4 *